HOW TO BE A
GLOBAL
CITIZEN

HOW TO BE A
GLOBAL
CITIZEN

BE INFORMED. GET INVOLVED.

Senior Editor Sreshtha Bhattacharya
Senior Art Editor Shreya Anand
US Editors Heather Wilcox, Lori Cates Hand
Project Editors Neha Ruth Samuel, Amanda Wyatt
Project Art Editor Mansi Agrawal
Editorial Team Bharti Bedi, Upamanyu Das,
Priyanka Kharbanda, Bipasha Roy
Art Editor Anukriti Arora
Assistant Art Editor Bhavnoor Kaur
Illustrator Mohd Zishan
Project Picture Researcher Deepak Negi
Picture Research Manager Taiyaba Khatoon
Managing Editor Kingshuk Ghoshal
Managing Art Editor Govind Mittal

DTP Designers Nityanand Kumar, Bimlesh Tiwary
Pre-production Manager Balwant Singh
Production Manager Pankaj Sharma
DK India Editorial Head Glenda Fernandes
DK India Design Head Malavika Talukder
Senior Production Editor Andy Hilliard
Senior Production Controller Meskerem Berhane
Jacket Designer Surabhi Wadhwa-Gandhi
Jacket Design Development Manager Sophia MTT
Head of Diversity, Equity, & Inclusion Lisa Gillespie
Publisher Andrew Macintyre
Associate Publishing Director Liz Wheeler
Art Director Karen Self
Publishing Director Jonathan Metcalf

This title was created with support from the DK Diversity, Equity, & Inclusion team.
Thanks to the Product and Content Working Group for their input and guidance.

First American Edition, 2021
Published in the United States by DK Publishing
1450 Broadway, Suite 801, New York, NY 10018

A catalog record for this book is available from the Library of Congress.
ISBN 978-0-7440-2995-6

DK books are available at special discounts when purchased in bulk
for sales promotions, premiums, fund-raising, or educational use.
For details, contact: DK Publishing Special Markets,
1450 Broadway, Suite 801, New York, NY 10018
SpecialSales@dk.com

Printed and bound in UAE

For the curious
www.dk.com

This book was made with Forest Stewardship
Council™ certified paper – one small step in DK's
commitment to a sustainable future. For more
information go to www.dk.com/our-green-pledge

CONSULTANTS

PHILIP BASELICE, MA
Philip Baselice, MA, is a Master Teacher at Nysmith School for the Gifted teaching US and World History. He also writes the history curriculum and teaches for the nonprofit Uplift Foundation, which helps make education accessible to all during the COVID-19 pandemic. He has previously lectured at Northern Virginia Community College. His history specialities include nationalism and cultural nationalism, authoritarianism, decolonization, the Cold War, and modern American and World History.

ROGER BRIDGMAN
Roger is an electronics engineer and was Curator of Communications at the Science Museum. He has written widely on the history of technology and lives in London with his wife and two guinea pigs.

TERESA DAY, MSC, RGN, RMN
Teresa Day trained and qualified as both a general nurse and a mental health nurse. She has spent most of her career working in the field of adolescent health, including carrying out research into relationships and sex education for her Masters dissertation. In her current role she supports and trains school staff, specializing in emotional health and well-being, and relationship education.

DR. TONY JUNIPER, CBE
Dr. Tony Juniper, CBE, is an internationally recognized campaigner, writer, sustainability adviser, and environmentalist. For more than 30 years, he has worked for change toward a sustainable society at local, national, and international levels. A regular speaker and participant at international conferences and symposia, he has also authored and coauthored numerous books about our changing environment, including multi–award-winning best sellers. He has held a number of senior roles, including Executive Director of Friends of the Earth, Executive Director at WWF, President of the Wildlife Trusts, and advisor to HRH The Prince of Wales.

PROFESSOR PAUL KELLY
Paul Kelly is Professor of Political Theory at the London School of Economics and Political Science and former Pro-Director. He is the author, editor, and co-editor of 17 books. His main interests are contemporary political philosophy, international political theory, and British politics and ideas.

DR. MEGAN TODD
Dr. Megan Todd is a senior lecturer in social science at the University of Central Lancashire, England. She has been teaching sociology in Higher Education for nearly two decades. Her research focuses on sexualities, gender, and violence. She has published on issues relating to intimate partner violence, aging, health, feminism, and homophobic and misogynist abuse online.

CONTRIBUTORS

ANDREA MILLS
Andrea Mills is an award-winning author who has written more than 50 children's and family reference books across a broad range of subjects, from animals and atlases to science and society.

BEN FFRANCON DAVIES
Ben Ffrancon Davies is a writer and translator based in Wales. He mostly works on nonfiction for children and adults.

SHANNON REED
Lecturer, University of Pittsburgh, and author of *Why Did I Get a B? And Other Mysteries We're Discussing in the Faculty Lounge*.

A NOTE ON HERITAGE, RACE, AND ETHNICITY
In this book, we capitalize Black when talking about race. This is part of our use of capitalized adjectives describing identities related to ethnicity and race (apart from "white"). We do this because these adjectives represent historically marginalized communities with common cultural identities. This includes the capitalization of Black, Hispanic, Indigenous, Aboriginal, and Native American, as well as the typical capitalization of nationalities and identities such as German or Asian.

Other organizations have begun to capitalize white along with other racial identities, but we use lowercase in this book. Some commentators suggest that calling attention to whiteness through capitalization can be a tool for recognizing the systematic privilege it confers. However, "White" does not carry the same sense of shared history and culture imbued in terms such as "Black" or "Indigenous." The capitalization of white is also often used by white supremacists to indicate racial dominance. For these reasons, DK is choosing to not capitalize white.

Contents

Our world

UNDERSTANDING OURSELVES
AND EXPLORING THE WORLD AROUND US

66 No one is born a good citizen; no nation is born a democracy. Rather, both are processes that continue to evolve over a lifetime. Young people must be included from birth. A society that cuts off from its youth severs its lifeline. **99**

Kofi Annan (former UN secretary-general), World Conference of Ministers Responsible for Youth, Lisbon, Portugal, 1999

Knowing yourself

As you grow up, you discover how all the different parts of you come together in one unique package to form your identity. You learn more about yourself and who you are as a person.

Understanding identity

Some parts of your identity may be clear at an early age, while others may develop as you grow older. It may take you some time to fully discover who you are, and your identity continues to change throughout your life.

> We know what we are, but not what we may be.
> **William Shakespeare** (English playwright), *Hamlet*, 1599–1601

What makes you "you"?
Everything about you is the reason you are unique. Although it is impossible to record every characteristic you have, a combination of features, such as personality type, values, interests and hobbies, family and cultural background, and gender and sexual identity, comes together to form your identity, which makes you different from everyone else.

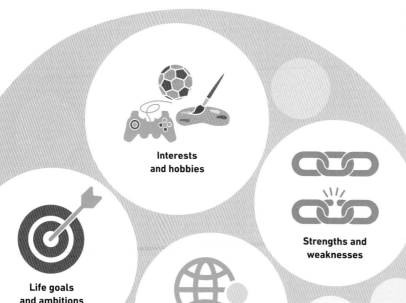

Interests and hobbies

Strengths and weaknesses

Life goals and ambitions

Cultural background

Support network of family and friends

Gender and sexual identity

I AM...

Personal values

Your values are the beliefs and principles you care about that influence the choices you make and the way you act in everyday life. Your values are usually influenced by your family, friends, teachers, and community. Everyone has a set of values—for example, that it's important to be respectful, kind, honest, and fair. Some people may believe certain values are more important than others, and the values you think are important now might change as you get older. Thinking about your values each time you have to make decisions will help you feel that you are being true to yourself.

Thinking independently
Listening to different viewpoints helps you think independently and make informed decisions on your own. Learning about other points of views can help you understand other people and expand your knowledge of the world.

Empathy and kindness
Empathy is the natural ability to understand how others are feeling. Showing compassion and kindness helps you to form trusting and lasting relationships, since everyone appreciates being understood and cared for.

Respecting others
You'll meet people from all walks of life. Respect and accept their identities and ideas just as you would like them to accept you. Whoever they are and wherever they come from, they have feelings too.

Managing peer pressure
Friends can have a big influence on how you think and behave. Sometimes you might feel pressure to act differently or change who you are to fit in. Remember, it's okay to be different and to say no or leave the situation if you feel uncomfortable.

Staying healthy

Looking after yourself and your body will help you have a happy, healthy mind too. If you eat well, get enough sleep, try to be kind to yourself, and take time to do the things you enjoy, you'll be much better equipped to tackle the challenges of everyday life.

Talk to someone

If you're feeling overwhelmed, don't be afraid to talk about how you feel to a trusted adult, such as a parent or a teacher at school. If you need more help, you can try speaking to your school counselor or a doctor to help you manage your feelings.

Physical well-being

Eat healthy foods
Eating a varied and balanced diet that includes proteins, grains, fruits, vegetables, dairy, vitamins, and minerals gives your body essential nutrients, boosts your energy levels, and improves your concentration.

Exercise regularly
Whatever sport or physical activity you enjoy, regular exercise helps you develop muscle and bone strength. Exercise also causes your brain to release endorphins—chemicals that make you feel happy.

Mental well-being

Accept yourself
Self-acceptance is learning to embrace all the different aspects of yourself, including the ones that you feel need improvement. It can be tricky, but try to appreciate who you are and what you have, and talk kindly to yourself, just like you would to a friend.

Simple pleasures
Making time for hobbies and interests can help boost your mood. Whether it's reading a book or going for a walk, take time to do the things you enjoy.

Relationships and feelings

The relationships you have at home, at school, or out in your wider community can provide support and create a safe space where you can talk about your feelings if you want to. As you get older, it's normal for these relationships to shift and change.

SEE ALSO	
❰ **10–11** Knowing yourself	
Living in a community	**14–15** ❯
Find out more	**151** ❯

Responsibilities

As you grow up, you become more aware of your role at home and might start sharing responsibilities with your family members. The more responsibilities you take on, the more independent and valued you feel.

Relationships

For relationships to stay happy and healthy, mutual understanding and respect are essential. Whether you are talking to close family members or making new friends, be open-minded, listen, and avoid making judgments. Above all else, try to be kind. Investing time and effort will help create relationships that can last a lifetime.

Responsibilities at home
Your schoolwork and study time at home are important for your education, while sharing in the household chores makes a difference to your family.

Homework and studies are your responsibility to keep up to date.

Your friends
Friendships often start because of shared interests. When you make an emotional connection with someone, it often leads to a longer relationship and mutual respect.

Doing chores, such as laundry or cleaning, are essential to running a household.

Looking after pets is a big responsibility. If you have a pet, it will need to be fed and taken care of.

Your family
Families come in different sizes. Children may live with one parent, two parents, grandparents, or aunts or uncles. Your older relatives can share their own knowledge and experiences.

Intimate relationships
During your teenage years, you may form special relationships in which you become emotionally and physically close to another person. In this type of relationship, both people must give consent and respect boundaries.

Big life changes

At some point, families may face unexpected or life-changing events that can be very unsettling. Among the biggest changes are moving to a new home, parents separating or getting divorced, a family member or friend becoming seriously ill, or a loved one dying. Anything on this scale can have a huge impact on all family members. It can take time to accept a new situation and adjust after a difficult event, but share your feelings with someone close to you if you want to.

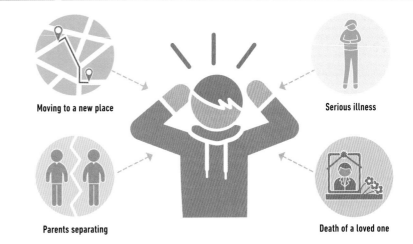

Moving to a new place

Serious illness

Parents separating

Death of a loved one

Managing feelings

Sometimes, you may struggle with your feelings. You may feel content and calm one minute but angry or sad the next. These changes in feelings are completely normal. They can be the result of what is going on inside you or what you are experiencing around you. Talking about your feelings with someone you trust, such as a family member or a friend, can help.

Physical changes

Your feelings can be affected by lack of sleep or changes in your body due to puberty. Both can make you more tired, highly emotional, and unable to think clearly. This may lead to angry outbursts, mood swings, and headaches. Getting plenty of rest should help you manage these problems, but if you're finding things difficult, be sure to speak to someone you trust or visit the doctor for help.

Seeking help

Sometimes your emotions can feel overwhelming—whether it's stress before an exam or frustration with your family. It might be difficult to talk to someone about your feelings, but speaking to trusted family or friends can help. If you continue to feel overwhelmed, seek professional help from a school counselor or a doctor to help you deal with difficult feelings.

Handling your stress

Challenges in everyday life may leave you feeling overwhelmed and stressed. A little bit of pressure can be motivating, but too much is exhausting physically and mentally. There are lots of things you can do individually or with family and friends to help you manage any stressful feelings.

• Take some deep breaths, which can help you feel calmer in the moment.

• Try to take a break from whatever is making you feel overwhelmed. Time or space away from what makes you stressed will help you calm down and think more clearly the next time you tackle the problem.

• Ask someone you trust for tips on how they deal with stress and what helps them relax.

• Play a sport, watch a movie, or do something else you enjoy.

Living in a community

Everyone around you makes up your community. Beyond your immediate circle of close family and friends are your neighbors, classmates, teachers, and other social groups. A sense of community is built by people living and working well alongside each other.

Know your community

As you grow up, you learn to get along with all sorts of people by interacting with those in your community. Just a short conversation in passing may result in new connection! Knowing the members of your community can help you feel more at home in your local area.

If you want to go quickly, go alone. If you want to go far, go together.
African proverb

Community life
For individuals, feeling part of a community creates a positive atmosphere and can boost general well-being. In a strong community, citizens feel connected and comfortable with each other. Some communities may be closer than others.

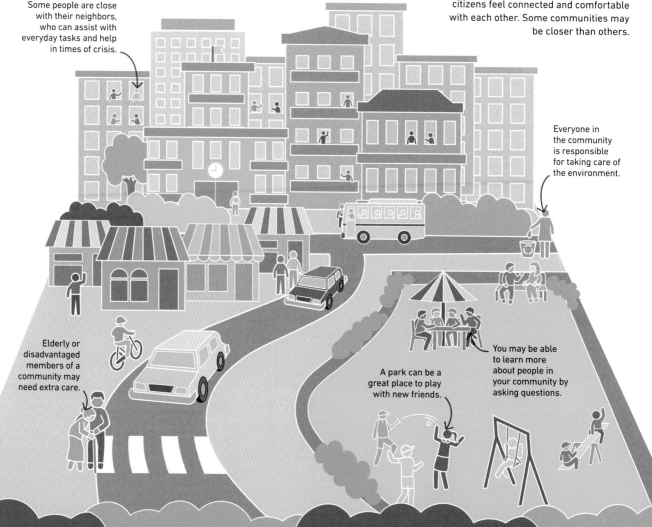

Some people are close with their neighbors, who can assist with everyday tasks and help in times of crisis.

Everyone in the community is responsible for taking care of the environment.

Elderly or disadvantaged members of a community may need extra care.

A park can be a great place to play with new friends.

You may be able to learn more about people in your community by asking questions.

Interacting with your community

There are many different ways to build relationships in your community. You might say hello to the bus driver or talk to the cashier at your local store. You may meet someone in your community with shared interests or a similar background or who goes to the same school. These interactions help create a sense of community spirit as well as helping your own communication and development.

Help everyone

If someone in your community needs help, make a point of reaching out to them. Your actions show that a support network is in place to benefit everybody.

Stick to your values

Approach others with kindness, respect, and empathy, the same way you would want someone to interact with you. When meeting new people, remember to be accepting and friendly. People in your community will notice your positivity and hopefully treat others the same way.

Connect with others

Get to know people from different backgrounds in your community. People may look or behave differently, but accept everyone as they are and avoid making judgments. A community of diverse members keeps things interesting and inspiring for all its members.

Manage conflict

If you're arguing with a friend, it might be hard to stay calm. Continuing to be angry and upset could make the argument worse. Remember to take time to listen to what your friend is saying and to respond to them respectfully.

Peer pressure

Everybody is influenced by their friends, in positive and negative ways. Sometimes, you might feel that you need to behave or dress in a particular way to fit in. This influence is known as peer pressure. If you ever feel uncomfortable about what your friends are doing or asking you to do, it's okay to say no and to change the subject or leave the situation. Think about what is best for you and know that it's okay to be different.

Bullying

Bullies hurt others mentally or physically. Make sure you reach out for support if you are the one targeted by bullying, or if you feel pressured by peers to target others.

Who is a citizen?

A citizen is a member of a country in which they were born or where they live. In many countries, mostly democracies, every citizen has rights, responsibilities, and a say in how their country is run.

Understanding citizenship

Individuals can gain the citizenship of a country, or become its citizen, in different ways—for example, by birth, by moving to the country and staying there for a period of time, or by seeking safety in the country. Citizens of a country may belong to many different groups, and they are expected to get along and behave respectfully toward each other. Citizenship of a country can inspire a sense of unity, belonging, and pride among people. There are lots of ways for citizens to support the values of their communities and make a difference in society.

Responsibility

Each citizen has responsibilities in society—both personal and public ones. Learning about these responsibilities can help citizens carry them out easily.

Respect

Good citizens show respect for others in the community by honoring the wishes and feelings of those around them. They also respect the laws of the country in which they live.

Compassion

Compassion motivates an exceptional citizen to care for the well-being of other people and living things around them. It encourages them to support those who might need help.

Tolerance

Tolerance means realizing that everyone is entitled to their opinions and beliefs. A good citizen respects and appreciates the differences between individuals and those between groups of people in society.

Honesty

A good citizen knows that being honest with others is the right thing to do. Honesty helps build trust between citizens.

Courage

Being courageous isn't always easy, but sometimes being a good citizen means standing up for yourself and other people. It also means being a good ally to those who are discriminated against.

Rights and responsibilities

In a democracy, citizens have certain freedoms and rights, such as the right to education and access to healthcare. These rights are guaranteed by the country's laws. As well as these rights, citizens also have some responsibilities, including paying taxes and following the law. If a citizen commits a crime, their rights can be taken away.

RIGHTS

The right to freedom of thought and speech

The right to worship freely

The right to vote

The right to education

RESPONSIBILITIES

Abiding by laws of the country

Voting to elect your representatives in government

Respecting the rights of other people

Paying taxes

Contributing to your country

Citizens can help their country in different ways. They might choose careers that benefit others and make a difference in their communities. Citizens may also be involved in volunteer work to help individuals or groups of people in need.

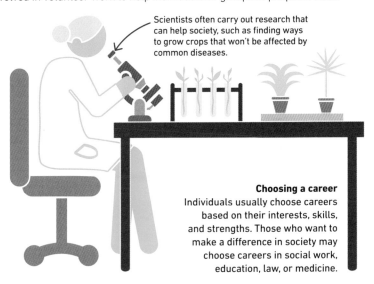

Scientists often carry out research that can help society, such as finding ways to grow crops that won't be affected by common diseases.

Choosing a career
Individuals usually choose careers based on their interests, skills, and strengths. Those who want to make a difference in society may choose careers in social work, education, law, or medicine.

Is everyone equal?

While all citizens living in a country should have equal rights and opportunities, this is often not the case. Some groups of people may be marginalized and face discrimination due to aspects of their identity, such as their race, ethnicity, religion, or gender identity. Their rights may be limited by unfair laws, and discriminatory policies may deny them the same opportunities that others have. These problems may force some people to leave their country for another, where they may have the opportunity to become citizens.

Are we global citizens?

The world has become a smaller place—distant locations are a plane ride away, and the Internet has allowed us to connect with people around the planet. By working together as global citizens to tackle the challenges faced by humanity, we can all help make the world a better place.

Global citizenship

Global citizenship goes beyond national borders to unite people as members of humanity. Global citizens are aware of what's happening in the world, they care for each other, and they understand that today we are all interconnected more than ever. They have an appreciation for different ways of life and respect for diversity. As global citizens, we have to work together toward solving common problems, such as climate change, pollution, racism, poverty, and wars. The idea of global citizenship can encourage people to take action locally, nationally, and globally to build a more tolerant, diverse, sustainable, and peaceful world for everyone.

One world
Citizens across the world are connected in many different ways. These links go beyond national borders and stretch worldwide.

Thinking globally

Because of how interconnected the world is today, your actions can affect people beyond your own community. Things you do in one place can positively or negatively affect those living far away. Try to be thoughtful about your actions and find ways to help or support others. These efforts can range from buying local produce that will benefit area farmers to raising your voice against injustice in another country by supporting a movement.

International trade and economies link communities and countries together as a global workforce.

Environmental issues are a common concern for people, regardless of where they live.

We should be united when facing our common problems.

To truly be global citizens, we must embrace cultural diversity and accept all beliefs and ideas.

Being respectful, considerate, and truthful is just as important online as it is in the physical world.

Raising awareness

As you learn about global issues that need attention, try to find a cause that interests you and talk with your family and your community about it. Share your knowledge and find out what you can do about the issue.

Taking initiative

Your local community is the starting place for action. Join forces with like-minded people, build up support for your cause, organize fundraising efforts, and work together to make a difference for those in need.

Creating an impact

As a global citizen, you can unite with others locally, nationally, or globally for a common cause. Your efforts can help people in need, even if they are on the other side of the planet.

The Internet connects people online as one big, global community.

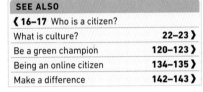

It is our responsibility to take care of the planet and adopt more sustainable ways of living.

Meeting people from different backgrounds and experiences adds to our understanding of the wider world.

Modern transportation allows people to travel all around the world for work and enjoyment.

Our society

TACKLING BIG ISSUES AND FINDING OUR PLACE IN SOCIETY

" We may have different religions, different languages, different colored skin, but we all belong to one human race. **"**

Kofi Annan (former UN secretary-general), statement made as the chairman of the Kofi Annan Foundation, 2016

What is culture?

Culture is the way of life shared by a group, a community, or a nation. It can influence almost everything people think, do, or have in society. A shared culture brings people together, creating a sense of belonging.

SEE ALSO

❰ **14–15** Living in a community
❰ **18–19** Are we global citizens?

Discrimination	**28–29** ❱
Celebrating differences	**50–51** ❱
On the move	**86–87** ❱
Communicating online	**130–131** ❱

Understanding culture

Culture includes the values and beliefs, customs and traditions, objects, languages, art, and history shared by a group of people. We are all affected by the culture we grow up in. Culture changes over time, and it is influenced by people traveling to and experiencing other places or by seeing other cultures on television or the Internet.

Languages
People of an ethnic group often speak a unique language, which is an important part of their cultural identity.

Values and beliefs
Religious or spiritual beliefs, as well as family values, may influence the identity of an individual.

CULTURE

Art
Art and artistry capture the traditions, beliefs, and lifestyles of groups of people from different periods of time.

Customs and traditions
Traditional practices followed for generations reflect the unique identity of an ethnic group.

Objects
Traditional clothing, historical artifacts, and jewelry are cultural symbols that provide a shared meaning to people.

History
A shared history affects the beliefs and values of people in a community and how they live.

A multicultural world

As people move around the world to live, they may share aspects of their culture with others while also experiencing the culture of their new community. Many countries now have a mix of cultures, with groups of people from different backgrounds living alongside each other, sharing beliefs, ideas, and traditions. Having a better understanding of cultural similarities and differences can give us a greater appreciation of the world and all the people in it.

Multicultural neighborhoods give people the opportunity to experience different cultures—for example, by eating food from different parts of the world.

People from different cultures bring new skills and ideas that can improve businesses.

Children growing up in a community with diverse cultures may be inspired to learn more about the wider world.

Types of culture

By focusing on different aspects of culture, we can break it down into four different types: national culture, lifestyle culture, ethnic culture, and religious culture. A person's identity is often influenced by a combination of these four different types of culture. For example, someone's national or ethnic culture may influence the language they speak or the festivals they celebrate, their lifestyle may inform the clothes they wear or the music they listen to, and their religious culture may determine their diet or their moral values.

We can thrive in our own tradition, even as we learn from others, and come to respect their teachings.

Kofi Annan (former UN secretary-general), Nobel Lecture, 2001

Type	Description
National culture	This type is linked to people's sense of belonging to a nation. It consists of shared languages, beliefs, traditions, food, festivals, and symbols that are significant for most people of the country.
Lifestyle culture	Lifestyle culture describes how people express their personal values and beliefs through the way they live. It may include how they dress, what music they listen to, and other interests, such as avoiding plastic or meat.
Ethnic culture	People of a certain ethnicity may develop specific practices or customs over time, which form their ethnic culture. It can include traditional clothing, social customs, and a unique language, for example.
Religious culture	Religion has always had a huge impact on the culture of people and places. Religious beliefs affect many aspects of life, such as clothing, diet, family values, and rituals at different life stages.

Cultural spaces

Public places, such as markets and parks, show glimpses of our multicultural world. They provide opportunities for people of different cultures to come together and interact.

Everyday conversations can help people of different cultures become more considerate and understanding toward each other.

Activities such as sports can cross cultural divides and unite people in a shared experience.

Different challenges

People from different cultures may clash over beliefs or ways of living when they have trouble understanding, respecting, accepting, or learning about one another. If people of a culture in the majority value their own traditions so much that they dismiss others, then people who are a minority can be left feeling oppressed, and they may face discrimination, racism, and violence because of their cultural identity. Governments can help promote multiculturalism—they can educate students about the different cultures in a country, support different cultural groups by recognizing more national holidays, encourage everyone to respect all cultures, and take steps to stop discrimination, racism, and violence against specific groups of people.

Is everyone equal?

Equality is the idea that every member of a society, regardless of their race, ethnicity, gender, sexual identity, or abilities, should have the same status, rights, and opportunities and be treated in the same way.

Achieving equality

In an equal society, everyone would have the same rights and be treated with equal respect, with nobody being treated less favorably than anyone else. Unfortunately, inequality exists almost everywhere in the world. Until unfair treatment of people based on stereotypes and prejudices is tackled, unequal access to rights and opportunities will continue to be a problem for many.

> As long as poverty, injustice, and gross inequality persist in our world, none of us can truly rest.
> **Nelson Mandela** (former South African president), London, UK, 2005

Equal opportunities

In an ideal society, differences would be acknowledged and celebrated, and all citizens would have the same opportunities regardless of who they are, what they believe, or where they are from.

Is equality enough?

Equality aims to treat everyone exactly the same, but this approach can still leave some people at a disadvantage due to their particular needs. Equity acknowledges that everyone needs help with different things and that adapting support to match a person's unique situation is the best way to make sure that everyone has the same, fair access to opportunities.

Equity

Treating people with equity means offering support specific to each individual's situation. A shorter person might need more help in reaching for an apple on a tree in the same way that some children might need extra help from a teacher to do their homework.

EQUALITY

When the whole group is given exactly the same help in the form of the same boxes, the taller individuals still have an advantage over the shortest person, who cannot reach the apples.

Deciding who gets the boxes means that each individual is offered help specific to their needs. Everyone is raised to the same height, meaning that they now all have equal access to the apples.

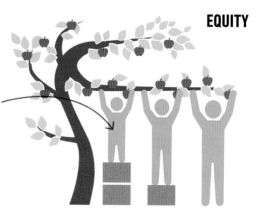

EQUITY

Equity in society

It is important for equity to exist in every part of society so that everyone has fair and equal access to the same opportunities. No one should be held back from achieving their full potential in life. Here are some ways to help create a society that is more equitable.

Employment
Employers can put policies in place to make sure that everyone's circumstances are taken into account, such as flexible working hours for parents with young children. This means that people from all communities have the chance to succeed and be represented at all levels of a company, and more employees are able to reach their full potential.

Public spaces
Public spaces, such as transportation, parks, and museums should be easy to use for everyone. Ensuring that people of all abilities can enter and exit the space easily makes these spaces inclusive for everyone.

Healthcare
Healthcare needs to be accessible to everyone. For example, some people may need help to travel to a hospital, and others may need appointments at certain times of the day due to work schedules.

Education
Providing free education to everyone is only the first step. To ensure that every student has the opportunities they need to succeed, their individual circumstances and needs must be addressed. Some students may need information presented in different ways for them to fully understand it.

Government policies
Government policies should take additional care to address the needs of groups that are underrepresented or discriminated against in order to make sure that all areas and aspects of society are inclusive of everybody.

Inclusion champions

CHANGE MAKERS: MARGINALIZED GROUPS

Many young advocates are highlighting the issues faced by people who have been displaced, rural and indigenous communities, and other marginalized groups. Their work helps those most in need.

Jasilyn Charger

A member of the Cheyenne River Sioux Tribe, American indigenous environmental advocate Jasilyn Charger was 16 when she joined the battle against oil pipelines on her community's lands. Jasilyn saw that young people of indigenous communities (culturally and ethnically distinct people native to a particular region of the world) needed to support each other. She co-founded the International Indigenous Youth Council to support the education of young indigenous people.

Rayanne Cristine Máximo Franca

Since the age of 17, Rayanne Cristine Máximo Franca has worked for the empowerment of indigenous women in Brazil. As part of the Indigenous Youth Network, she has spoken out about the lack of equality for indigenous women in healthcare and education. In 2015, Rayanne helped collect and report the concerns of indigenous women across the country, which led to the creation of the Brazilian government's first-ever national agenda for indigenous women.

Heidy Quah

Malaysian social rights champion Heidy Quah founded Refuge for the Refugees, an organization that aims to provide better standards of education and healthcare to refugee children. In recognition of her work, Heidy became the only Malaysian ever to receive the Queen's Young Leader Award in 2017.

Sohini Shoaib

Queer feminist campaigner Sohini Shoaib fights for the rights of some marginalized members of Indian society. Working with an organization called Jan Jagaran Shakti Sangathan, she has brought attention to the economic and social problems faced by farmers, laborers, women, LGBTQ+ people, and those from India's oppressed castes.

India Logan-Riley

After specializing in Maori history and archaeology, India Logan-Riley went on to become a key member of Te Ara Whatu, an indigenous youth climate group based in New Zealand. She has attended UN climate talks to pursue her dream of ensuring that indigenous voices are heard and considered in the fight against climate change.

Mohamad Al Jounde

Syrian refugee Mohamad Al Jounde is one of the most outspoken champions for the rights and welfare of refugee children. At the age of 12, he built a school in a refugee camp in Bekaa Valley, Lebanon, with the help of his family and volunteers. His efforts won him the annual International Children's Peace Prize in 2017. Today, he works with children who have endured wars and trauma and helps them express their emotions through art and photography.

Mohamad Al Jounde with children in a refugee camp in Lebanon

Discrimination

When someone is treated unfairly because of one or more aspects of their identity—such as their age, race, and sexual or gender identity—it is called discrimination. It is a result of unfair prejudices and stereotypes.

Understanding discrimination

The person discriminating usually belongs to a majority group and considers themselves superior or typical. Those who suffer discrimination may be part of a minority group, and they may find themselves mistreated, bullied, denied opportunities, and also excluded from situations or groups. Discrimination can cause people to feel scared, isolated, confused, or angry, and it often leads to inequality and reduced rights for a group. There are many types of discrimination. Sizeism, for instance, is discrimination because of a person's body size.

Looking at ourselves

Sometimes a lack of personal awareness and understanding can lead to discrimination happening without people realizing. Ask yourself whether you ever treat people differently—unintentionally or deliberately—based on your own prejudices. Try to be aware of the prejudices you have.

Classism
Discrimination against people because of their social class includes prejudice based on their job, income, or the place where they grew up.

Casteism
This involves dividing people into social groups in a hierarchy. The people placed lowest in the social order may be treated unfairly.

Ageism
Prejudice regarding age can affect both young and old. Assumptions can be made about what a person is capable of based on their age.

Intersectionality

The different parts of a person's identity in society, such as race, ethnicity, class, gender, and sexual identity, may combine to produce unique forms of discrimination for an individual. This combination of factors affecting a person's experience of discrimination is known as intersectionality. It may affect a person overwhelmingly as they are treated unfairly for many parts of their self at the same time.

Sexism

Racism

Classism

A working-class Black woman may experience greater discrimination because of her gender, race, and social status.

> The way we imagine discrimination...is more complicated for people who are subjected to multiple forms of exclusion.
> **Kimberle Williams Crenshaw** (US law professor), Netroots Nation conference, Atlanta, Georgia, 2017

Racism
Discrimination because of someone's race or ethnicity is racism. Race is a social idea that divides people based on physical traits such as skin color, while ethnicity relates to the shared social, cultural, and historical experiences of a group of people.

Religious discrimination
Judging an individual or group because of their faith or religious beliefs is a form of discrimination.

LGBTQ+ discrimination
This involves treating someone differently or being offensive or aggressive toward someone because of their sexual or gender identity.

Sexism
Discrimination against someone on the basis of gender identity usually affects women more than men.

Ableism
This is faced by disabled people or people with abilities different from what is perceived by some as "normal" or "typical."

What are stereotypes?

Oversimplified ideas about individuals or groups are called stereotypes. These are often a set of assumptions made about every member of a particular group. Stereotypes are widely held, and they may form in people's minds without them even realizing it. This is called unconscious bias.

GET INVOLVED

Break the cycle

If you see or hear about discrimination going on at school or in your community, try to show your support for the person who is being discriminated against. Talk about it with a trusted adult, such as a parent or a teacher.

This person might wrongly assume that all Muslim women dress in the same way because of their religion.

This person might wrongly assume that all disabled people need a lot of help.

Stereotypes in action
Opinions formed about strangers based on just one aspect of their identity can strengthen prejudices and reinforce inequality in society.

What is ableism?

Ableism is a form of prejudice or discrimination against disabled people and against persons with abilities different from what is perceived as normal or typical by able-bodied people.

Disability

A disability is a physical, mental, or sensory condition that may be temporary or long-term and can affect how a person carries out their everyday activities. More than one billion people in the world have some form of disability. The spectrum of disability ranges from ones that can be seen to those that are not visible. People with the same disability often have different experiences and points of view about it.

Visible disabilities

Some physical disabilities are referred to as visible—this means that they can be seen by others. Disabilities of this type may restrict a person's body in some way, affect mobility, or limit the senses. These disabilities can be present at birth or result from accidents or illnesses.

Invisible disabilities

People can have disabilities that are hidden and can't be seen by others. Many of them are related to the nervous system and brain, and some are chronic conditions present from birth. They include diabetes, chronic pain, sleep disorders, mental illness, and learning difficulties.

Understanding ableism

Ableism is a type of prejudice and discrimination faced by disabled people. It wrongly assumes that able-bodied people are more "normal" or superior to those with disabilities. Examples may include when assumptions are made about what disabled people can and can't do, or when negative language is used to describe disabled people or disabilities. Ableism and the unfair favoring of able-bodied people can present themselves in many different ways in society and leave disabled people feeling frustrated and excluded.

Physical ableism
A lack of clear information in buildings and public places can make it difficult for disabled people to move around independently.

Social ableism
This is when the incorrect assumption is made that there is only one way for all people, including disabled people, to learn or do things—for instance, making a child with a reading disability read aloud for practice, even if they don't want to.

Cultural ableism
Disabled people are often described either as inspirational or tragic figures. The disability of an athlete may be discussed more than their achievements.

Looking at disability

When thinking of how disabled people can fully participate in their communities, an ableist perspective may assume that a disabled person would want to find a medical solution for their disability if they could. A more equitable approach—when people's differing needs are recognized—accepts disabilities for what they are and suggests changes in communities, such as buildings with better access and signage, that would make it easier for disabled people to fully participate.

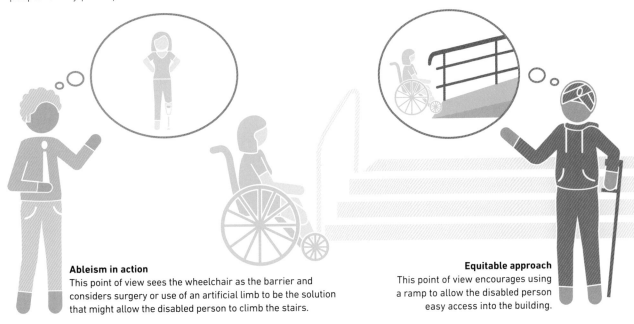

Ableism in action
This point of view sees the wheelchair as the barrier and considers surgery or use of an artificial limb to be the solution that might allow the disabled person to climb the stairs.

Equitable approach
This point of view encourages using a ramp to allow the disabled person easy access into the building.

Ending ableism

In order to stop ableism, it's essential to treat disabled people with respect. Disabled people may not need, or want, help, sympathy, or questions about their disability. One way to be supportive is by recognizing disabled people as unique individuals not defined by their disability.

GET INVOLVED

Avoid ableist language

Many words and phrases, such as "idiot," "dumb," "cripple," "retarded," "slow," and "insane," are examples of ableist language, and we may end up using these casually without realizing that they may have damaging and discriminatory effects.

Show respect
Treating everyone the same way, with respect and dignity, is the best way to interact with those around you, whether they are disabled or not.

Women's rights

Historically, men have held greater power than women in society. For centuries, women have been campaigning for equal rights, resulting in positive changes that are still being built on today.

A struggle for rights

In the past, only men were able to own property, to get an education, and to vote. Women around the world, throughout history and still today, have fought to gain the same rights in society as men. The problem of gender inequality is not yet solved, and people around the world are continuing to try to improve women's positions in society. Gender equality allows everyone the opportunity to achieve their full potential—it is a basic human right. Additionally, studies have shown that countries experience greater economic growth if women are equally empowered.

Right to education
The fight for equal education in the mid-19th century led to many countries allowing education for everyone. However, in some parts of the world, there are still many girls who can't access education.

> Each time a woman stands up...she stands up for all women.
>
> **Maya Angelou** (American poet), endorsing Hillary Clinton, 2007

Right to vote
Until the early 20th century, only men were allowed to vote. Even though women in most countries now have the right to vote, there are many places where women struggle to do so.

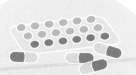

Right over one's body
In some countries, women do not have the right to choose if and when to have children. They may have limited or no access to contraception or legal abortion. These restrictions can be dangerous for a person's mental or physical health.

Key reform movements
Since the 19th century, women have overcome many obstacles in the fight for gender equality. Today, in most countries, women have the right to vote and access to education, but there are many places where these goals are still to be achieved. Not all women face the same challenges, and some groups face more challenges than others—transgender women, for instance, may face additional prejudice and discrimination.

Right to equal pay
In 1979, the United Nations adopted the Convention on the Elimination of All Forms of Discrimination Against Women. Despite this, women around the world continue to receive less money than their male counterparts for the same work.

Sexism

Prejudice and discrimination against a person because of their gender identity, carried out usually by men and boys mostly against women or girls, is called sexism. Women and girls can encounter sexist behavior at school, on the streets, at work, or even in politics. Sometimes, sexist attitudes are expressed as hate speech, misogyny (hatred against women), and even violence.

Sexual harassment
This kind of sexual harassment includes a range of behaviors, from making unwelcome comments or jokes about others to unwanted touching or physical violence, based on aspects of the target's identity, such as appearance, clothes, or behavior. Behaving in this way toward people is never acceptable.

Menstruation

Every month, people with a uterus may experience a biological process known as menstruation, or a period, when blood is discharged from the uterus. Not every woman has periods, and not every person who has periods is a woman. Historically, people have avoided talking about periods, but they aren't something to be embarrassed about. In parts of the world, women and girls are made to feel ashamed about having periods. Others may not be able to access information about menstrual products or easily buy them, or even find private, hygienic spaces to use them.

Unequal representation

In almost every area of society, women are largely underrepresented. From politics to sports and entertainment, there are fewer women employees, particularly at the top levels. Having more women in decision-making roles—for example, in politics—means that decisions are more likely to benefit everyone in society, not just a select few.

At the top
Even when women climb the career ladder, they may be unable to reach the highest positions due to discrimination still prevalent in male-dominated workplaces. This is changing slowly.

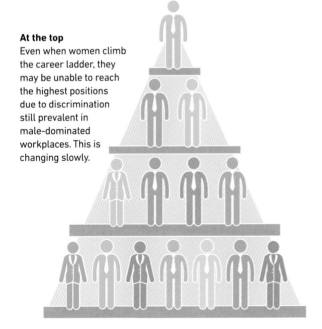

Feminism for all

Feminism refers to the view that men and women should be treated equally, and it is also the name given to the movements that work to address women's inequality in society. Feminists believe that women should have equal rights to men. You don't have to be a woman to be a feminist—anyone can be! Historically, feminism has focused on the lives of white, heterosexual women in Europe and the US, and so the voices of women of color and other groups have often not been heard. Fortunately, this is starting to change. Intersectional feminism includes the experiences of all women and recognizes that different parts of a person's identity—including race, sexual identity, and class—may create additional obstacles in their struggle for equality.

Global feminism
Women's rights movements must strive to encompass those from all walks of life and all different backgrounds to create a balanced and more equal world.

Champions for women

CHANGE MAKERS: WOMEN'S RIGHTS

A new generation of young champions is empowering women and girls all over the world. These educators and advocates are campaigning for gender equality and equal opportunities, while challenging societies dominated by men.

Malala Yousafzai

Pakistani teenager Malala Yousafzai (second from left) is a campaigner for girls to have access to education. In 2013, she co-founded the Malala Fund with her father. This organization supports education for girls in many countries. In 2014, Malala became the youngest person ever to receive the Nobel Peace Prize.

Malala stands with Nigerian schoolgirls in 2014.

Qabale Duba

Starting out as a nurse in Kenya, Qabale Duba went on to establish a community-based organization called the Qabale Duba Foundation (QDF). It works to empower young African women in rural communities by providing better education and health services. As well as leading literacy programs for Kenyan women, Qabale also donates underwear and menstrual products to schoolgirls.

Marley Dias

Disappointed by a lack of books featuring Black girls in her school library, American teenager Marley Dias launched a campaign called #1000BlackGirlBooks in 2015. Marley aimed to collect 1,000 books with a Black girl as the main character and donate them to schools. Her campaign showed the need for books with a diverse range of characters that represent all readers, not just some.

> There are two powers in the world; one is the sword and the other is the pen. There is a third power stronger than both, that of women.
>
> **Malala Yousafzai**, *I Am Malala*, 2013

Amika George

Concerned that many girls miss school due to a lack of menstrual products, British student Amika George started the #FreePeriods campaign. The government responded to her request for free menstrual products and agreed to stock schools in England with enough supplies.

Angellica Aribam

Indian political campaigner Angellica Aribam founded the Femme First Foundation, which promotes female leadership in politics by providing training and mentorship. Politics in India is overwhelmingly dominated by men, but Angellica is working to turn this around by encouraging young women to follow a political career.

Beliefs and faiths

There are thousands of different faiths around the world, which offer their followers sets of beliefs and principles to guide them through life. There are also many people who choose not to believe in any religion.

SEE ALSO

‹ 16–17 Who is a citizen?

‹ 22–23 What is culture?

‹ 28–29 Discrimination

Celebrating differences **50–51 ›**

Faiths around us

Most religions usually involve the worship of a higher being in the form of one god or many gods. For some people, religion is the spiritual beliefs they hold dear—these beliefs may influence and affect all aspects of their lives. Embracing religion can create a sense of order for some people and help them build bonds with others who follow the same faith. Many countries have different belief systems, but some have only one main faith. In large parts of the world, people are free to practice the faith they choose.

Belief systems

Belief systems range from ancient ones, such as paganism, to modern faiths, such as Scientology. The major belief systems around the world have millions of followers, with the largest ones followed by over a billion or two. However, there are also many people who are either unsure about their beliefs or who do not follow any religion.

Hinduism
Originating in southeast Asia more than 4,000 years ago, Hinduism is one of the world's oldest religions. Its followers, the Hindus, worship many gods and goddesses. Their religion is based around teachings and philosophies outlined in ancient texts.

Islam
In the 7th century CE, Islam was founded in the Arabian Peninsula. In this faith, the Prophet Muhammad is the messenger of the one true god, called Allah. Muslims (followers of Islam) believe in Allah's words as revealed in their holy book, the Quran.

Judaism
Dating back nearly 4,000 years, Judaism is an old religion. The followers of this faith, the Jews, trace their origins to nomadic people called the Hebrews. They believe in one God, and their teachings are collected in the Hebrew Bible, which is the Jewish sacred text.

Sikhism
The spiritual leader and teacher Guru Nanak founded this faith in the 15th century CE in Punjab, a state of modern-day India. The followers of Sikhism, the Sikhs, live by his teachings and those of nine other spiritual leaders.

Atheism
The followers of this system, called atheists, range from those who deny that a divine power exists to those who don't believe in one.

Christianity
The world's biggest religion has more than two billion followers called Christians. Their beliefs are based on the birth, life, death, and resurrection of Jesus Christ—believed to be the son of God. Their sacred book, the Bible, collects the teachings of Jesus and other prophets.

Buddhism
This religion was founded in the 6th century BCE by Siddhartha Gautama, who later came to be known as the Buddha. The followers of this religion, known as Buddhists, seek to achieve enlightenment, or a state of inner peace and wisdom, by following the Buddha's teachings.

Agnosticism
This is the belief that the existence of a divine power can never be proven beyond all doubt, so it is impossible to commit to one faith.

Religion and identity

An individual's beliefs and faith are a part of their identity. Followers of the same religion often feel they have a shared identity. Devout believers may consider their religious ideals to be more important than any other beliefs they hold. An individual's view on religion may evolve over time. For instance, a child's understanding of religion at a young age may be shaped by the belief system of the family. As they grow older, the child may question those beliefs and eventually may even choose a different faith.

Conflicting beliefs

Conflict can sometimes arise between followers of different religions who do not share the same beliefs. Religious intolerance can create distrust and even hatred between people, leading to tensions and divisions in society. Intolerance of other faiths may result in some people adopting extreme views and rejecting other beliefs completely. This is called religious extremism. If anyone you know is expressing extreme views, speak to a trusted adult, such as a parent or a teacher.

Religious intolerance
Intolerance can cause neighbors to make no effort in trying to understand each other's faiths.

Understanding each other

Regardless of whether people are born into a religious family or follow no faith, it may be helpful for them to learn as much as they can about different faiths. Considering the ideals central to each religion and the similarities they share may be more useful than focusing on any differences. Understanding religion may be a personal experience, but seeing another faith in practice through someone else's eyes can make it easier.

> I believe in God, but not as one thing.... I believe that what people call God is something in all of us.
>
> **John Lennon** (English singer-songwriter), 1966

Read up
Reading about different religions and faith systems around the world creates a deeper understanding of them.

Talk to people
Speaking to followers of other religions gives one a greater understanding of the values that are important to their faith.

Experience other cultures
Visiting friends during religious festivals, if they are open to it, could be a good way to learn more about their beliefs.

Racism

Racism is the wrong belief that certain races, ethnicities, and skin colors are superior to others. Racism is everywhere, and although the situation is improving, there is a long way to go before everyone is treated equally.

Understanding racism

Racist views can be held by individual people, but they may also be ingrained into an organization, a community, or an entire society. These views can be the result of unquestioned assumptions, ignorance, hatred, fear, and the belief that certain people are inferior or superior to others. Racism can be expressed in many different ways, from racist insults and workplace discrimination to racially motivated hate crimes and the state-sponsored racism that brought about the Holocaust during World War II. On a personal level, racism is damaging to the dignity, happiness, health, and opportunities of people who are forced to experience it. At a societal level, it can lead to policies and laws that are unequal, unfair, and discriminatory.

Personal prejudice

Personal prejudice is when someone judges someone else based on their race, ethnicity, skin color, or any other trait. This can be an intentional choice caused by ignorance, hatred, or fear, or it can come from unconscious bias, which is when you make assumptions about a person without even realizing it. In a job interview, a manager's prejudices may cause them to prefer one candidate over another based on their race or ethnicity.

Terms	Definitions
Race	Describes a way of classifying people based on their perceived physical differences such a skin color.
Ethnicity	Describes the shared social, cultural, and historical experiences of a group of people.

Stereotyping

When someone assumes that all people who belong to a certain group have the same traits rather than consider them as individuals, they are stereotyping those people. The unethical police tactic of racial profiling, which means believing that someone is more likely to commit a crime because of their race, is a result of stereotyping.

BE INFORMED

Apartheid

Apartheid was a social system in South Africa that separated people based on race and skin color. It was based on the idea of white supremacy—the misguided belief that white people are superior to other races. Its aim was to keep the white minority in power and marginalize all others, particularly the Black majority.

Systemic racism

Systemic racism is a type of racism that becomes common in a society usually after a long history of laws, policies, and social attitudes that maintain racial inequality. Systemic racism often leads to social inequality—for example, Black communities in the US have historically often lacked access to good housing.

Types of racist behavior

Racism can be expressed in many different ways, and some types are more obvious than others. Racist behaviors such as violent hate crimes that happen out in the open are the easiest to spot, but there are many other more subtle examples, such as the use of microaggressions.

Unconscious bias
Racist, stereotypical, or discriminatory views or actions that people hold or carry out without even realizing.

Racial profiling
When people suspect that someone is more likely to have committed a crime based on their race or ethnicity.

Microaggressions
Subtle actions or comments based on stereotypes that create a hostile environment for those experiencing them.

Police brutality
When police officers use unnecessary force against civilians. Some races or ethnicities may be subjected to it more often than others.

Racial slurs
Extremely offensive insults that use words and phrases that mock a person's race or ethnicity.

Hate crimes
A crime committed against a person because of a part of their identity, including race or ethnicity.

Symbols of hatred
Graphic signs or symbols that represent a hateful point of view, such as the Nazi swastika.

Housing discrimination
Racial discrimination that makes it difficult for people of some races or ethnicities to find suitable and affordable housing.

Hiring discrimination
Racial discrimination that makes it harder for people of some races or ethnicities to get hired.

Racist jokes
Jokes that use offensive and culturally stereotypical ideas about certain races or ethnicities.

Effects of racism

For people who experience it, racism can be tiring and upsetting and have devastating consequences. Racism can have a serious impact on a person's self-esteem and confidence and can endanger their physical safety, health, and well-being. It can also negatively affect the access to opportunities that a person has later in life.

White privilege

White privilege means that white people often have an advantage over those of other races or ethnicities. Many white people do face difficulties in life, but white privilege means that the color of their skin isn't an additional barrier like it might be for others in a similar situation.

Social and economic problems
Racism creates economic and social inequality, such as limited access to jobs, education, healthcare, and housing.

Health issues
Racism puts people at higher risk of physical harm but can also affect their mental health, leading to stress, anxiety, and depression.

Internalized racism
Racist attitudes can become so accepted within a society that the very people targeted by them may start to believe that they're true.

» I have a dream that my four little children will one day live in a nation where they will not be judged by the color of their skin but by the content of their character.
Martin Luther King Jr. (Black civil rights leader), *I Have a Dream* speech, 1963

Colorism in action

There tends to be greater representation of lighter-skinned people in media and film. This can become a never-ending cycle—for example, as lighter-skinned people are seen more frequently in the media, it may reinforce the belief that lighter skin is more "attractive" or normal." Broadening representation of people of all skin colors in the media would help combat colorism.

What is colorism?

Colorism is a type of racism in which people, usually from the same race, are treated differently because of how light or dark their skin is. It is based on untrue assumptions about what is considered desirable or attractive. From the 17th century onward, when European powers took over countries in some parts of the world, lighter skin became a symbol of superiority, which had an impact on people's views on lighter and darker skin. Those with darker skin may have fewer opportunities in education or employment than those with lighter skin because of colorism.

How can we overcome racism?

Racism is a huge problem all around the world, and there is no easy solution. There is still much to be done, but progress is gradually being made. The UN's Universal Declaration of Human Rights declares that nobody should be discriminated against on the basis of their race or skin color, and many countries have made racism illegal. But declarations and laws alone won't solve the problem—in order for society to become more equal, people need to take responsibility for recognizing and overcoming their own personal prejudices.

Laws and policies
Government policies and anti-discrimination laws can help tackle issues such as workplace inequality and make sure that everyone has equal access to housing and healthcare, regardless of race or ethnicity.

Raising awareness
Educating people about the effects of racism and encouraging them to imagine how it can make someone feel can inspire people to challenge their own prejudices or call out racism when they see it.

Personal attitudes
It may be hard to confront family and friends about racism, but talk to them when you feel ready. This can give you the confidence to engage other racist members of your community to help them recognize their prejudices if it is safe to do so.

Sexual identity

Sexual identity is just one aspect of who a person is, and no one should be defined by it. Understanding this part of yourself can take some time and may be a bit more confusing for some people than it is for others.

What is sexual identity?

Sexual identity is about more than just sex. It is part of a person's sexuality—the feelings, thoughts, preferences, behaviors, experiences, and beliefs they have relating to sex and sexual attraction. Sexual identity describes how a person identifies themselves based on who they are attracted to emotionally, romantically, and sexually and how they express these attractions. It's a very personal thing and can be an important part of who they are. Not only might someone's sexual identity play a part in defining how they see themselves; it can also influence how society sees them too.

Asexual/Ace
This term describes someone who experiences very little sexual attraction or none at all. They may or may not form romantic connections.

Lesbian
This term refers to a woman who is attracted to other women. "Gay woman" and "lesbian" are sometimes used to mean the same thing.

Gay
This term refers to people who want to be romantic and potentially sexual with people of the same sex.

Aromantic
This word describes someone who doesn't want to be in romantic relationships. They may or may not have sexual relationships.

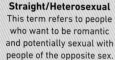

Straight/Heterosexual
This term refers to people who want to be romantic and potentially sexual with people of the opposite sex.

Bisexual
This usually describes someone who is attracted to both men and women but can refer to attraction to any other two genders or a range of genders.

Queer
This umbrella term can be used to describe a wide range of LGBTQ+ identities. Not all LGBTQ+ people identify as queer, though.

Types of sexual identity

There are many different sexual identities, and someone may identify with more than one of them. For example, a person may identify as both asexual and aromantic. For some people, their sexual identity is clear to them from a young age, while for others, it may take time to become clear. No one has to decide on a particular label—it's up to the individual to decide what is right for them.

Pansexual
This term refers to an individual who may be attracted to any other person, regardless of that person's gender.

Understanding sexual identity

Discovering their own sexual identity is harder for some people than for others. Some people never question their sexual identity, whereas others take time to understand how they feel.

Your sexual identity
Don't worry if you are not certain what your sexual identity is. Take the time you need to explore this part of yourself. You don't have to tell people how you feel if you aren't yet ready to.

Coming out
If you identify as LGBTQ+, telling your family and friends about your sexual identity, or "coming out," can be daunting. If and when you're ready, sharing this part of your identity and confiding in someone you trust can be a huge relief. Nobody should feel pressured to come out if they don't want to.

The problem of heterosexism

Heterosexism is the assumption that everyone is straight—this stems from the prejudiced belief that heterosexual people are "normal," while LGBTQ+ people are "abnormal." For LGBTQ+ people, it can be frustrating to have to repeatedly correct the assumptions people may make about them. Heterosexism can occur at an individual level, such as when someone assumes that a teenage boy has a girlfriend when he actually has a boyfriend, or at a societal level, when the news fails to report stories affecting LGBTQ+ people.

Untrue assumptions
When someone assumes that everyone is straight, it can make LGBTQ+ people feel as if they need to hide who they really are.

Celebrating sexual identity

Throughout history, many LGBTQ+ people have had to hide their sexual identities out of fear of social rejection, punishment, and even persecution. Sadly, some people must still hide their sexual identity, but in many parts of the world, it has become safer to be open about it. Events such as Pride parades celebrate the LGBTQ+ community, helping show that everyone should be proud of who they are, no matter what their sexual or gender identity is.

LGBTQ+

LGBTQ+ stands for Lesbian, Gay, Bisexual, Trans, and Queer or Questioning. The + represents the many other sexual and gender identities not covered by these letters. This term is used to refer to the entire community of people who identify as any sexual identity other than straight or as any nonbinary gender identity. Other versions of this acronym also exist with different letters to specifically include other sexual and gender identities.

BE INFORMED
Homophobia

Homophobia is the fear or hatred of LGBTQ+ people. People with homophobic views often believe that anything other than heterosexuality is morally wrong. This fear and ignorance makes them discriminate against LGBTQ+ individuals. In some countries, there are even laws preventing people from being their true selves. Attitudes are gradually changing, and there has been global progress for LGBTQ+ rights in recent years, but homophobia is still widespread.

Gender identity

When babies are born, they are assigned a biological sex, usually either male or female. People may assume that a person's gender matches the anatomy they were born with, but gender identity is more complicated.

What is gender identity?

A person's gender identity can be a combination of the biological sex they were assigned at birth, who they feel they are, and how they express themselves. While biological sex is a description of a person's anatomy, gender is the traditional set of expectations that society has about how a person should look and behave.

Biological sex
This describes a person's physical characteristics or anatomy. Most people are assigned either male or female at birth. Some people are born intersex, which means they have characteristics of both sexes.

Gender identity
This is the gender that a person feels represents them, and it may or may not match the sex they were assigned at birth. It's about whether a person sees themselves as a man, as a woman, or as another gender. No one else can say what another person's gender identity is.

Gender expression
This is how people express their gender identity outwardly. A person's gender expression may not always match their gender identity if they are not yet sure of or able to express their true self. Gender identity can change over time.

Different identities

Gender is often thought of as binary—a system with two parts, "male" and "female." In reality, gender (like sex) is nonbinary (not limited to two parts). There are many ways for people to describe how they identify, some of which are included here. People may use these terms differently, as there is no single agreed-upon meaning for any of them.

Cisgender
When someone's gender identity is assumed to match, without problems, the biological sex they were assigned at birth.

Transgender
A person who identifies as a gender that doesn't match the biological sex they were assigned at birth. For example, someone who was assigned "male" at birth may identify and live as a woman.

Agender
Also known as genderless, lacking gender, or gender-neutral, this term is used by people who don't see themselves as any particular gender.

Pronouns

These are words like "he," "she," and the gender-neutral "they" that are used in place of someone's name. People can choose the pronouns that best reflect their gender identity. If you're not sure of someone's pronouns, it's best to politely ask.

Gender stereotypes

Gender stereotypes are commonly held ideas about how people in society should dress, behave, and act based on traditional expectations about masculinity and femininity. Unfortunately, if people don't conform to these expectations, they may encounter disapproval from others. When the media portrays stereotypical ideas about gender in society, it can lead some people to feel there are things they can't or shouldn't do or to feel pressure to act in a certain way. No one should feel as if they are limited by what society expects of them. Questioning and challenging gender stereotypes can allow everyone, regardless of their gender, to achieve their full potential, free from outdated expectations.

In the 21st century, women in many parts of the world have opportunities to take on jobs—such as ones in construction—historically taken mainly by men.

Exploring your gender identity

Understanding their gender identity is harder for some people than it is for others. Some people may experience gender dysphoria, which is the emotional distress a person experiences when their body doesn't match their gender identity. It's okay to spend time exploring your gender and who you are and for your gender identity to change throughout your life. It can be difficult to talk about, but if you are feeling upset or anxious, share your feelings with someone you trust or reach out to a doctor, counselor, or support organization for help and advice.

Questioning
Someone who is undecided about their identity and who doesn't want to commit to a specific label.

Gender-fluid
A person with a changing range of gender identities. They don't consider their gender to be fixed. Their gender may vary at different times or in different circumstances.

Genderqueer
Also known as nonbinary, the word genderqueer covers a wide range of gender identities. This term is used by people who don't see themselves as either a man or a woman. They may identify as both, neither, or any other combination of gender identities.

Androgynous
This term is used to describe the gender expression of someone who blends traditionally masculine and feminine characteristics. Androgyny usually refers to how a person physically expresses themselves through clothing, hairstyles, and makeup.

LGBTQ+ champions

CHANGE MAKERS: LGBTQ+ RIGHTS

In many countries, people are discriminated against for their sexual and gender identities. Leading the way in the fight against this type of discrimination are the many young people championing equal rights for those in the LGBTQ+ community.

Jazz Jennings was Grand Marshal in the New York City Pride parade in 2016.

Jazz Jennings

One of the youngest people to publicly identify as transgender, American YouTube and television personality Jazz Jennings was featured in the American reality show *I Am Jazz*. This documented her life and the challenges she faced growing up as a transgender teenager. A champion for LGBTQ+ rights, Jazz co-founded the TransKids Purple Rainbow Foundation in 2007. The foundation helps transgender and gender nonconforming people by creating awareness and acceptance in society.

Ose Arheghan

While still at school in Ohio, Ose Arheghan started campaigning for a safe and inclusive school environment for LGBTQ+ students. Ose identifies as gender nonconforming, nonbinary, and queer. This young champion uses the nonbinary pronouns "they" and "them." Recognized for their work, Ose received the title of Student Advocate of the Year at the 2017 GLSEN Respect Awards.

Emi Salida

British YouTube personality Emi Salida came out as asexual (someone who is not sexually attracted to others) when she was 16 years old. To raise awareness of this sexual identity, Emi decided to talk about it on her YouTube channel. Emi's goal is to make asexuality more visible in the LGBTQ+ community.

BE INFORMED

GLSEN

Started by a group of American educators in 1990, the Gay, Lesbian, and Straight Education Network (GLSEN) is an organization that works to combat discrimination, harassment, and bullying of LGBTQ+ students because of their sexual and gender identities in schools in the US. It aims to create inclusive and supportive learning spaces for young LGBTQ+ people.

Amanda Bosco

Ugandan transgender advocate and human rights defender Amanda Bosco helps out grassroots communities through the African Queer Youth Initiative. This organization strives to give young people the freedom to express their sexual and gender identities without fear. Amanda works to defend the rights of transgender people in Uganda and support those suffering from HIV and AIDS.

Rukshana Kapali

Human rights campaigner Rukshana Kapali belongs to the indigenous Newa community of Nepal. She writes blogs and books about gender, sexuality, and indigenous rights. After working for two years in the Blue Diamond Society, an LGBTQ+ rights organization in Nepal, she co-founded the Queer Youth Group in 2019. This group for young people raises awareness of and champions rights for the LGBTQ+ community in the country.

What is marginalization?

Marginalization happens when certain individuals or groups of people in a society are treated unequally and given only limited access to the rights, resources, and opportunities enjoyed by the majority of the population.

SEE ALSO

❰ 28–29 Discrimination

❰ 30–31 What is ableism?

❰ 32–33 Women's rights

❰ 38–41 Racism

Be an ally   56–57 ❱

Sidelined by society

Although all citizens should be entitled to equal respect and treatment, this is not always the case in reality. When people are ignored or overlooked, discriminated against, and made to feel as if they have been excluded from society because of factors relating to their identity, it is known as marginalization. Marginalization can affect people due to their gender, sexual identity, culture, religion, physical abilities, race, or ethnicity. People who are marginalized often face a number of challenges, ranging from unequal rights to a lack of employment opportunities. While the challenges experienced by marginalized groups are starting to be acknowledged, much more still needs to be done by governments, citizen groups, and individuals to raise awareness, change policies and practices, and make everyone feel included in society.

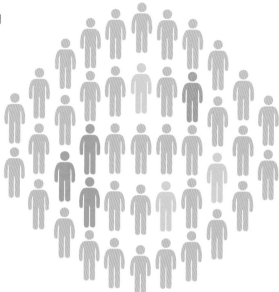

What contributes to marginalization?

An individual or an entire group may face being marginalized because of one or a combination of identity-related reasons, such as age, class, sexual or gender identity, race, religion, culture, ethnicity, or physical abilities. Being seen as unimportant, inferior to or different from what is considered "normal" by the majority of the population, or those in power, can result in people experiencing unfair social exclusion.

Historical factors
A group that has been marginalized in the past may still face discrimination today. The Dalits—who form the lowest caste in India—have been oppressed by the dominant castes for centuries.

Identity
Key factors that make up one's individual identity, such as gender, sexual identity, religion, race, or ethnicity are common reasons for marginalization and discrimination in society.

Cultural background
Some people are marginalized because their cultural backgrounds are different from the dominant cultures of a particular place. This includes refugees and asylum seekers who are new to a host culture.

Effects of marginalization

Marginalized people can face poor treatment and lack of recognition in society every day. Marginalization can cause hardships for individuals or groups of people, such as inadequate housing, poor living conditions, lack of access to healthcare, and economic inequality.

Basic needs
Marginalization can leave individuals and communities without basic essentials, including food, water, shelter, and clothing.

Health issues
People may face health issues due to poor living conditions or because their medical needs are ignored. It may also be difficult for them to access quality healthcare.

Economic problems
Lack of employment opportunities creates a cycle of poverty, from which people may struggle to escape.

Systemic discrimination
People from marginalized groups are often targeted by law enforcement. They may also have difficulty getting financial and legal support.

Protecting the marginalized

National governments, local communities, and individual citizens can all play their part in ending unfair treatment and protecting the rights of marginalized groups in society. There are many different ways this can be achieved, provided everyone makes a combined effort.

- Government policies should aim to be inclusive, so that marginalized groups have their needs met and do not suffer discrimination.

- Governments can boost employment opportunities for the most disadvantaged groups in society by empowering them with training programs and skill development courses and by creating new jobs.

- Citizen groups can help marginalized people by generating community support and raising donations to fund access to public facilities, education, and basic healthcare.

- On an individual level, people can make an effort to educate themselves on the struggles faced by marginalized communities by discussing the issues with these groups and do their best to be strong, supportive allies by listening carefully to those affected.

Economic factors
In capitalist societies, where profit and finances are the main motivations for growth and development, the most disadvantaged communities in society can be excluded and exploited.

Poor governance
Government policies in most countries take into account the needs of a vast majority of the population but often fail to address the problems and issues that directly affect marginalized groups.

Lack of access
The combined impact of social and economic inequality and the lack of equity result in individuals feeling cut off from resources and opportunities, which widens the gap between mainstream society and the marginalized.

Celebrating differences

In an ideal world, everyone would be included and diversity—the differences in their identity, background, or experiences—would be celebrated. But we still have a long way to go to achieve equality and respect for all.

What are diversity and inclusion?

The world is made up of people with all sorts of identities, backgrounds, and experiences. Diversity is when this variety is present in a society, and inclusion is when all these people are treated equally and fairly. This is often not the case in reality, as discrimination and inequality make it hard to have diverse and inclusive societies.

Coming together

While diversity and inclusion may be hard to understand, imagining a set of jigsaw pieces may help. Having a set of jigsaw pieces in different colors would mean diversity in the set. Inclusion is when they all fit together to form one multicolored shape.

Diversity

Inclusivity

Why diversity and inclusion are essential

By working together toward diversity and inclusion, we can create a society where everyone benefits. When people from every group are treated with sensitivity and respect, then nobody feels like they are left out or undervalued by society. There are many reasons why diverse and inclusive societies are better for all. Here are some of those reasons.

Equal opportunities
Everyone would have access to the same opportunities in life and would be treated fairly and equally.

Empowering people
Supporting other people and their needs would help create an environment where everyone feels like an equal member of society.

Stronger communities
A community where members get to know each other is one in which people may find it easier to trust and help one another. Learning more about the backgrounds, cultures, and life experiences of each other would make people more understanding of their differences.

Building a more inclusive world

All levels of society, from individuals right up to national governments, can play their part to build a more inclusive world. Inclusive societies can help reduce inequality by improving everyone's standard of living through better access to essential public services, such as education and healthcare.

Resources
Public resources should be distributed fairly to ensure that members of all groups in a community have access to such facilities as libraries, schools, and hospitals, no matter where they live within a city, town, or village.

Opportunities
Inclusive classrooms and workplaces offer everyone the same opportunities and allow all people the freedom to express their views and be heard. Listening actively means engaging with what's being said and taking the time to understand it.

Attitudes
Inclusive, welcoming attitudes can create safe spaces where people feel able to engage openly with each other. Encountering a wide range of cultures and experiences might help people become more supportive to others and stand up for them when necessary.

GET INVOLVED

Read a lot

Reading books by a wide range of authors who come from different walks of life and cultures can help you achieve a greater understanding of the world. Ask your teachers where you can find diverse reading material. Talk to your friends to see what they are reading.

We will all profit from a more diverse, inclusive society.
Ruth Bader Ginsburg (American judge), *My Own Words*, 2016

Fresh perspectives
A diverse society would bring together different perspectives from people with different experiences. This could help enrich the society.

Learning more
When students from diverse backgrounds come together, it could create opportunities to learn about cultures and experiences different from their own.

Productive workforce
A diverse workforce could be better at solving complicated problems because people with different life experiences would bring a wider range of ideas to the table.

Power to the people

A movement is a large group of people with shared beliefs coming together to make their voices heard on important subjects. Movements come about to bring a change in society.

Why movements happen

Movements are a powerful way for citizens to make a change, in addition to the actions taken by individuals and communities. In a democracy, when the government fails to take responsibility for its promises or citizens feel frustrated about an issue, people may choose to join a movement. A movement allows large groups of citizens to convey their demands to the government through collective action, such as petitions and protests. Some of the most significant moments in history were the result of movements.

Reformative movement
This type of movement aims to make specific, limited changes within the systems in a society, such as, for example, making demands that women have equal rights.

Revolutionary movement
This type of movement aims for fundamental, broader changes to systems in a society, such as removing a country's leader or entirely replacing the government.

Types of action

All movements involve action— from protests, strikes, sit-ins, and teach-ins to staging boycotts, signing petitions, or sharing hashtags. The actions taken can be peaceful, but some can turn disruptive. Occasionally, protests and marches can become riots, which are illegal. At times, people across the world unite at a particular moment for a shared cause as global citizens. In September 2019, a series of global strikes against climate change, known as Global Week for Future, were attended by people from 185 countries around the world—many of them students.

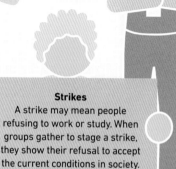

Protests
Protests and marches, when people gather together to make demands, show commitment to a shared cause and raise public awareness.

Group petitions
To express their feelings about a cause or situation, people may sign a petition on paper or online, asking the government or those in charge to make a change.

Strikes
A strike may mean people refusing to work or study. When groups gather to stage a strike, they show their refusal to accept the current conditions in society.

The power of social activism

In recent decades, movements set up to support particular causes have become more global, stretching beyond the borders of the country where they may originally have begun. This rise is fueled by the Internet and social media, where individuals and organizations can gather support internationally.

Student-led movements
It is common for groups of students to gather in support (or opposition) of a particular idea, such as during antiwar marches. They often use their large social networks to spread the word.

Civil rights movements
Some people in marginalized groups have become advocates fighting for civil rights. Movements such as #BlackLivesMatter help them fight for civil rights and freedom from discrimination.

Green movements
Some movements in the 21st century, led by organizations such as Greenpeace, are aimed at saving the rain forests, reducing pollution, fighting climate change, and protecting the environment.

Equal rights movements
These movements seek equal rights for everyone. Supported by organizations such as Stonewall, some of these movements focus on rights for LGBTQ+ people.

Teach-ins
People give lectures and debate on the causes that matter most to them, inviting others to join to build support.

Hashtags
The 21st century marked the start of online hashtag movements. They use the # symbol (used to collect content about a topic) to publicize support for different causes.

Boycotts
Another way to express discontent is to boycott a product, a company, or a country by refusing to buy or use their products and services.

Sit-ins
People can sit at a location and refuse to move until their discontent is acknowledged.

#BlackLivesMatter

CASE STUDY: SOCIAL MOVEMENT

One of the most powerful social movements of the 21st century started with people posting the hashtag #BlackLivesMatter on social media. The hashtag was used to highlight the unjust killings of Black people by police. Outrage at these killings led millions of people around the world to protest against racism and anti-Black police brutality.

Black Lives Matter

The slogan of the movement. It does not mean that other lives don't matter but that Black lives deserve respect.

What happened?

In 2012, a man named George Zimmerman fatally shot an unarmed Black teenager named Trayvon Martin in Florida. When Zimmerman was let go without punishment by the courts in 2013, there was an upwelling of anger among people. They began using the hashtag #BlackLivesMatter on social media in July 2013 to express their outrage over the racism, discrimination, and violence faced by Black people. Violent and fatal incidents continued to occur, including the murder of George Floyd in May 2020 by a police officer. Floyd's shocking murder brought more global attention to the #BlackLivesMatter movement. The hashtag once again went viral, and the slogan was frequently seen at protests and marches.

8.8 million
The number of tweets on Twitter that used #BlackLivesMatter on May 28, 2020, the most uses of the hashtag in a single day.

4,000+
The number of cities around the world where #BlackLivesMatter protests took place in 2020.

Marching for equality
On July 16, 2016, thousands attended a march in London, UK, to protest against racism.

Response
#BlackLivesMatter has made countries around the world examine how systemic racism and racial profiling have made Black people more likely to be treated unfairly. Some countries now recognize the need for changes to their police forces and justice systems.

Trayvon Martin's original memorial site, Florida

Why it happened?

The US has a long history of discrimination and violence against Black people. Trayvon Martin was a victim of this racial discrimination. The situation has been made worse by the repeated failure of the US justice system to punish white people when they are found guilty of crimes against Black people. The #BlackLivesMatter movement demands justice for these crimes, an end to racism, and changes in society that will ensure the equal treatment and safety of Black people.

Lessons learned

- **Creating awareness**
  This movement has drawn attention to the ongoing discrimination faced by Black people, not just in the US but around the world, and has highlighted the urgent need for change.

- **Action by everyone**
  Racism is everyone's problem to solve. We all have to try to make our communities equal and safe for all.

- **Hashtags raise awareness**
  Hashtags can unite thousands around a common cause. You can follow, share, or create hashtags to gather support for a cause.

GET INVOLVED

Be a better ally

Help combat racism by responding to hateful behavior when you see it, such as by speaking out against harmful language or racist jokes. An effective ally is supportive and listens respectfully and without interrupting to the stories of those who have experienced racism. With permission, share these stories to raise awareness of the problem.

Be an ally

Discrimination is a problem for everyone to solve, not just those who experience it. Being an ally means standing up for and supporting people who are treated unfairly because of who they are. Good allyship can help make our society more inclusive.

Who is an ally?

An ally is a person who has empathy and can imagine what problems someone else might face, what experiences they've lived, and how their lives might be different. These traits help an ally support those who are discriminated against or underrepresented, whether or not the ally experiences the same kind of hardship. Being an ally also means recognizing that you may enjoy privileges that some people do not have and using your privileges to support others who are treated unfairly. The act of being an ally, also known as allyship, allows all citizens to play a part in making society fairer for everyone.

How to be an ally

There are many things you can do to be an ally, from using social media to draw attention to underrepresented voices to raising money for causes that will support them. Being an ally isn't always easy, but by speaking out against discrimination and supporting those who face it, even when it gets challenging, you can make a real difference. When you want to help someone, make sure you find out first what kind of support they need, without making any assumptions or acting without their permission.

Speak out
If you hear someone in your family or friends saying something discriminatory, try to speak up if it is safe to do so.

Educate yourself
Learn about issues affecting the community you're supporting, such as misconceptions or hurtful language.

Listen
Listen to those who are at the center of the struggle. Ask them how you can provide support. Respect their decision if they don't need your help.

Get involved
Work with the people you're supporting, in the way they want. Find out and help with the tasks that will benefit them the most.

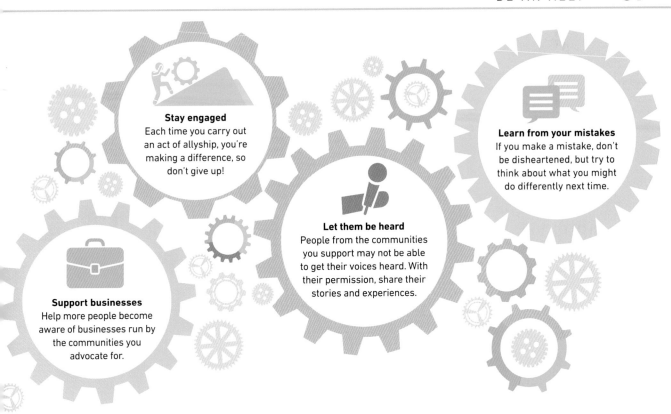

Stay engaged
Each time you carry out an act of allyship, you're making a difference, so don't give up!

Learn from your mistakes
If you make a mistake, don't be disheartened, but try to think about what you might do differently next time.

Let them be heard
People from the communities you support may not be able to get their voices heard. With their permission, share their stories and experiences.

Support businesses
Help more people become aware of businesses run by the communities you advocate for.

What is privilege?

Privilege is when someone has unearned social advantages over others based on certain characteristics, some of which never change, such as skin color, and others that can change over time, like how much money they have. It is possible for people to be privileged in some ways and not in others. People with privilege may find it awkward to talk about, but thinking about it may be the first step in becoming more aware of the inequalities in society. Using their privilege in a meaningful way can help an ally make a difference.

Harnessing privilege

True allyship goes deeper than just showing superficial support without doing much, which is known as performative allyship. Trying to help someone counts more than simply talking about the need to do so. For example, sharing a hashtag and talking about what needs to change is a great first step, but by acting on those concerns—by trying to volunteer to help those who need it—you can make a real positive difference.

I raise up my voice—not so I can shout but so that those without a voice can be heard.
Malala Yousafzai, "Youth Takeover of the UN" Youth Assembly, 2013

People and politics

HOW COMMUNITIES AND COUNTRIES GOVERN THEMSELVES

" Democracy gives us citizens a measure of political power. That power comes with a responsibility to foster a culture that makes it possible to live and work well together for the well-being of all. **"**

Diane Kalen-Sukra (Canadian author and motivational speaker),
Save Your City: How Toxic Culture Kills Community & What to Do About It, 2019

What is politics?

The word "politics" is often used when talking about how a country is run and who has power, but it is much more than that. Politics is the way any group makes decisions, discusses problems, and chooses to organize itself.

Understanding politics

Politics is all around us—from how households are run to our choices of leaders. It governs how all areas of society are managed, including education, the environment, and the economy. Politics allows us to make decisions on these topics as a group, even if not everyone agrees.

Politics in the family
Parents usually set rules for their children to follow. If you don't understand a rule, try to discuss it with a parent.

Politics in the workplace
Problems and conflicts in the workplace are handled by managers, who try to find solutions that work for all employees.

Politics in the government
Governments make rules and laws for everyone to follow. They have the power to decide how society is run.

Types of political systems

There are a variety of governments today with different types of leadership, each based on the kind of political system in their country. Nearly half of the world's countries are democracies. A democratic government is voted in by the citizens and is meant to act on their behalf.

Democracy
In a democracy, the citizens vote for their preferred choice of leader.

Oligarchy
A small number of citizens have power over a country, usually as a result of their wealth or influence.

Monarchy
The leadership is usually passed down through generations of a royal family, but the monarch may share power with a democratic government.

Dictatorship
One person holds power over the rest of the population and makes all the decisions.

Who forms the government?

In a democracy, citizens come together to elect their local, state, and national representatives. Citizens usually align themselves with one specific political party and vote for candidates running for political office who represent their preferred party. All the elected representatives join forces to form the government. It is their job to work on behalf of the people who voted them into power. If they don't, they will probably be voted out at the next election and lose their power.

Political parties
Citizens with similar political beliefs form parties with shared goals. They present their ideas to convince people that their party would benefit society the most.

Campaigning
Political candidates campaign to gather support in the run-up to elections. People usually vote for the candidate who most closely shares their views.

The right to vote

Most citizens in a democracy are given the right to vote. This is an important responsibility for every citizen because it determines how the country is run and who is put in charge. To cast their votes on Election Day, citizens usually go to polling stations and place a mark in the box of their preferred political candidate on the ballot paper. In some countries, citizens may also be able to vote early or mail in their votes.

What does a government do?

The government is responsible for maintaining law and order in society. It enforces existing laws, passes new laws, and uses courts of law to punish law-breakers. Among its other main functions are managing the economy and providing financial assistance where necessary, running public services such as schools and parks, and providing security and support in times of natural disasters or international conflict.

GET INVOLVED

Discuss and debate

Take part in discussions and debates at home and school to share your thoughts and hear different viewpoints. Watch congressional debates to see politics in action and think about who would get your vote.

We need to provide enough resources for our new renewable energy initiative.

Let us discuss our policy with everyone else.

Political systems

The series of rules about how a society is run and how its leaders are chosen form its political system. Every society needs a political system to function effectively.

Different systems

Created to organize society, political systems have evolved over time. Examples of old political systems that were common include monarchies and oligarchies (rule by a few). Today, many countries are democracies—political systems where governments are made up of representatives elected by the people. There are also countries run by a single person or political party, or even guided by a religion. No political system is perfect, and each has its own challenges.

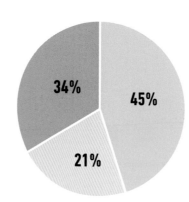

34% **45%** **21%**

KEY

- Democracies
- Mixed systems (including oligarchies)
- Authoritarian systems (including absolute monarchies and dictatorships)

Modern political systems
Published every year in the international newspaper *The Economist*, the Democracy Index lists how many countries are democracies and how many are not. According to the 2020 Index, 45 percent of all the countries in the world are democracies.

Democracy

In a democracy, citizens have the power to choose their leaders. They exercise this power by voting in elections. Democracies were first established more than 2,500 years ago in Ancient Greece, where citizens met to discuss how to run their communities and to vote on important issues. This type of system, known as direct democracy, allowed people to make their own decisions on policies. As populations grew over time, it became impossible to ask everyone's views on different issues. A new type of system called representative or indirect democracy evolved, wherein one person is chosen in an election to represent others and make decisions on their behalf.

Constitutional monarchy
In this kind of representative democracy, a monarch shares power with an elected government. The monarch has a limited role and follows the decisions of the government, which controls the day-to-day running of the country. Constitutional monarchies include Japan and the UK.

Japan UK

Federal republic
This is a type of representative democracy in which the national government shares power with the different regions or states in the country, which have their own elected governments. The prime minister or chancellor is the head of the national government, and the president usually has limited power. Germany and India are examples of this system.

Germany India

Monarchy

In this political system, a king or queen, known as a monarch, rules the nation. They usually inherit this position because they were born into a royal family and hold it for life or until they wish to step down. In most countries in the world today, the monarchies have transferred their power to democratically elected governments. But some countries have what's known as an absolute monarchy. In this system, the monarch controls the country and makes all the important decisions. This can be seen as a form of dictatorship by some.

Oligarchy

An oligarchy is a political system in which a small group of people hold all power in a country. These oligarchs rule according to their own interests. The government may be formed by people who were born into the aristocracy (a social class of wealthy, powerful people) or those who belong to a particular military, corporate, religious, or political group.

Government of the people, by the people, for the people.

Abraham Lincoln (former US president), Gettysburg Address, Gettysburg, Pennsylvania, 1863

Presidential republic

Citizens vote for the head of the government and their elected representatives in this form of representative democracy. In countries such as France, the president appoints a prime minister to run the government and shares power with them. In others, such as the US and South Africa, the president is the head of the government. The US is a federal presidential constitutional republic.

The US

South Africa

Dictatorship

Some countries are governed by a type of system in which one person has absolute control, often without a constitution in place. This is called authoritarianism. One example is a dictatorship—a system in which the ruler, known as a dictator, does not allow any opposition to their power or position. The country runs according to the interests of the dictator, and the citizens have no say in how they are ruled. Most dictators stay in power until they are removed by force or die.

Parties and elections

Citizens who share the same views can get together to form political parties. These parties then compete with each other in local and national elections to try to earn the majority of the public votes and win power.

Political parties

Every country has its own problems to solve and issues to debate. All the citizens in society have their own ideas and opinions about how this should be done. Political parties are formed by groups of citizens with shared views. The members work hard to gather support. Democratic countries may have candidates from one or more political parties vying for the citizens' votes in an election.

If you win, will you represent my community?

Yes, we will.

Public politics
Candidates discuss their policies at local meetings, such as town halls, and online forums. Citizens can get their questions answered and then decide which candidate wins their vote.

Political ideas

At the very heart of political parties are big ideas. These shared beliefs range from how the country should be run to what rights each citizen should have. These political approaches stretch from far left (a term used to describe Communism) to far right (a term referring to fascism). Between the far left and far right is everything else, including some moderate approaches.

> The right to vote freely for the candidate of one's choice is of the essence of a democratic society.
> **Earl Warren** (former chief justice, US Supreme Court), 1964

Far left	Left	Center	Right	Far right
Communism	**Socialism**	**Liberalism**	**Conservatism**	**Fascism**
In this system, the government is in charge of the country's resources. Citizens share everything equally, and no one owns anything privately.	In socialist societies, the wealth of the nation is shared evenly between the citizens by the state. The government is responsible for citizens' education, healthcare, and housing.	Liberalism emphasizes citizens' rights, freedom, and the same opportunities for all. It supports free trade and economic growth benefiting all citizens.	Conservatism seeks to avoid rapid changes. In this approach, the government's authority is seen as important for maintaining order, and private ownership of businesses is promoted.	In a fascist society, a dictator or supreme leader heads the government and has control over the country. A group of citizens of a certain race or nationality may be favored.

What is an election?

Elections are the process in which citizens vote to select candidates from political parties to represent them in the government or other political office. A citizen's decision about who to vote for depends on their personal political ideas and how much their own views are shared with those of a political party. In an election, the candidate with the most votes is declared the winner.

Campaigning
Political candidates from different parties campaign to convince the public that they are the best choice. They present plans about how they would run the country and bring about change.

Voting
On election day, voters cast their vote by choosing from the list of candidates. In some countries, they may vote early.

Campaigning for victory

A powerful campaign can influence people's opinions and bring in more votes. Political parties use a variety of tactics to attract voters and encourage support, but ultimately the ideas and information presented by the candidates determine whether people are willing to vote for them.

Meeting voters
Face-to-face meetings between citizens and candidates are a great opportunity for citizens to ask questions or share concerns they may have and for candidates to find out more about what potential voters want.

Sharing a vision
Each political party shares its policies and promises with potential voters. Some parties might have lots of policies covering all aspects of running society, while others might focus on a specific issue, such as the environment.

Campaigning events
At campaigning events, candidates make speeches and talk to groups of citizens about their policies and plans. They try to persuade citizens to listen to their ideas and potentially vote for them.

Debating issues
Candidates sometimes go head-to-head with current leaders in televised or radio debates. These debates are an opportunity for citizens to get to know the candidates better and compare the policies proposed by different sides.

Voting

In a democracy, citizens have the right to choose their leaders through voting. This is an important responsibility because voting allows citizens to play a role in deciding how their country is governed.

The right to vote

One of the most important features of a democracy is the right to vote. In an election, citizens have the power to choose who is in charge of their country. Elected leaders make decisions that affect everyone. In some countries, it is compulsory for eligible citizens to vote in elections, and this may be enforced by law.

Who can vote?
Most countries today have universal suffrage, which is the right to vote for all citizens ages 18 and above. In the past, some sections of society did not have the right to vote because of their gender, ethnicity, income, or social standing.

Why should you vote?
In a democracy, every single vote counts equally. Voting gives citizens the power to decide who represents them in government. In this way, citizens are able to shape decisions that their government might make.

Registering to vote
In the US, citizens must be registered to vote in their district of residence in order to vote in local, state, or national elections. It is important to register to vote as soon as you are old enough so you don't miss out on the opportunity to have your say.

Being a responsible voter

It is best to be informed before casting your vote. Find out whether the candidates in an election agree with you on various issues. Learn about their past history and voting record, what values and ideas they hold, and their party's policies and agenda. Look at the other parties campaigning and see which is most suited to your preferences.

Look for accurate information on the candidates and their policies on their official websites or party websites.

Know your candidates
There is usually plenty of information about candidates available to read online. By researching the policies of different candidates, you can find out what they think about issues you care about.

> Voting is not only our right, it is our power.
> **Loung Ung** (Cambodian-American human-rights advocate), 2018

GET INVOLVED

Practice voting

As a future voter, it is important to understand how elections work by practicing how to vote. You could try getting involved in your school elections or vote on school events or activities. School or community elections are a great way to experience voting firsthand and help you see how every vote matters.

Casting a vote

Despite having the right to vote, some people choose not to vote or forget about elections entirely. But democracy works best if everyone participates. Low voter turnout is often the reason why elections fail to bring about any change in government. In most democracies, there are generally many different ways to cast a vote, and it is usually very quick and easy to do. Most countries make voting as simple and accessible as possible to encourage citizens to cast their vote.

Many states in the US use paper ballots marked by hand, which are then counted by a computer/machine. The paper ballots are still collected and counted by hand in cases of a recount.

Other states in the US use BMDs or DREs to record votes. BMDs present an electronic ballot to the voter and create a paper ballot that can be read by a human after the voter makes their choices. DREs are computers that present an electronic ballot and record the voter's choices in the computer's memory.

In the US mail-in voting (or absentee ballots) are provided to those who cannot make to the polling booth in person on election day for a pre-approved reason.

Modern online voting facilities in some countries allow voters to vote on a computer or mobile device from the comfort of their homes.

Postal voting systems involve voters mailing their ballots ahead of Election Day.

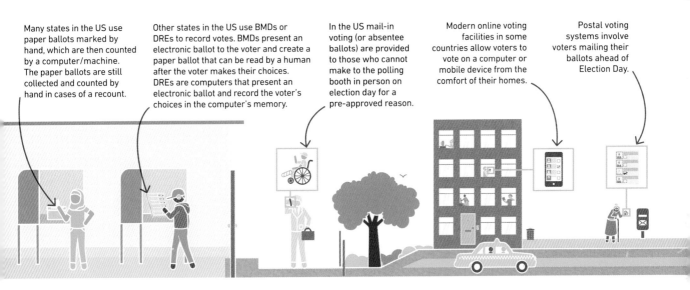

What happens to your vote?

Once all votes have been cast, they are then counted carefully. Most democracies use one of two electoral systems to decide the winner of an election. The plurality system sees the candidate with the most votes announced as the winner. The majority system means that a candidate must secure more than 50 percent of the votes to win. When choosing its president, the US uses a different system. The president is not directly elected by citizens. Instead, they are chosen after the popular vote in each state and the District of Columbia by by members of a body called the Electoral College, known as electors. Each state and the District of Columbia have a set number of electors and receive a certain number of electoral votes based on their representation in Congress, which is partly based on population.

The popular vote
Most elections in the US are decided by popular vote. In a presidential election, citizens vote for the candidates of their choice. After the votes are counted, every state and the District of Columbia determine which candidate won the popular vote for their state or the district.

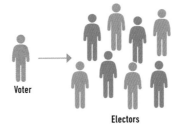

Voter

Electors

Electoral votes
In most states and in the District of Columbia, the party that wins the popular vote picks their chosen electors to cast all of the region's electoral votes for their presidential candidate.

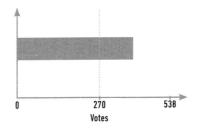

0   270   538
Votes

Deciding the winner
The votes cast by the electors are counted up by Congress. A candidate needs the votes of at least 270 electors out of 538, which is more than half, to win.

What is a government?

A government is a body that runs a country and organizes society based on different rules and laws for all the citizens to follow. In a democracy, a leader such as a president or prime minister is in charge of the government.

The government's role

A government provides order in society and helps run the country. It enforces existing laws and introduces new ones. It keeps the nation safe, with the support of the military, and is responsible for providing public services, which might include education, healthcare, policing, and public transportation. In a democratic country, the government is expected to consider the views of its citizens when making policies.

Constitutions

In a democracy, a constitution is the set of rules that describes how a country should be governed and what rights its citizens have. Some countries, such as the US, are governed by a written constitution, while others are guided by an unwritten constitution that is based on previous court judgments and actions taken by the legislature.

Functions of a constitution

- **Defines the role of the government**
  It describes the government's guiding principles and sets out the powers held by its branches.

- **Details the sharing of responsibility**
  It defines the extent of government rule and how responsibility is shared between national and local authorities.

- **Outlines the rights of the citizens**
  It describes the citizens' rights and freedoms.

Branches of government

In a democracy, the government is usually divided into three separate branches that work alongside each other to ensure the smooth running of the country. They function independently but may still deal with each other and provide checks and balances for one another. These branches are the legislature, the executive, and the judiciary.

◁ **Separation of powers**
No single branch of government holds all the power. Instead, power is divided between the three branches. This setup is common in democracies and is known as the separation of powers.

Legislature
Known as Congress in the US, this assembly of government workers passes legislation, which includes all the laws and rules. It may be divided in two parts in some countries.

Executive
Along with senior government officials, the leader of the executive branch executes (carries out) and enforces laws introduced by the legislature.

Judiciary
The judiciary interprets legislation in courts of law. Laws are applied to resolve disputes as part of a just and impartial legal system.

Head of government

In most democratic countries, the head of government is the highest position held in the executive branch of government. In many cases, the head of government is in charge of all government operations with the support of a cabinet of other key members in the government. This position may be held by a president, a prime minister, or even a chancellor.

Presidential system
As seen in the US, the president leads the executive branch but is chosen independently of the election of the members of the legislature. The president does not sit in the legislature.

Parliamentary system
As seen in India, in this system, the prime minister is the main candidate of the party that wins the most seats in the legislature in an election. The prime minister heads the executive branch and sits in the legislature.

Running a country

The government runs a country by working with its citizens, businesses, and industries. It gives its citizens rights, provides public services, and collects taxes from the citizens to fund its activities. In return, citizens have duties that they are expected to carry out. The government sets rules for businesses and industries, which in turn provide jobs that boost the economy.

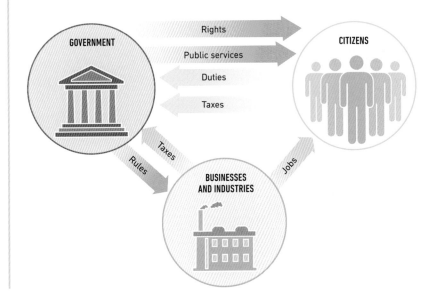

Sharing of power

National governments share power and responsibility with local and regional or state authorities to allow them to make their own decisions about what might be appropriate for their areas and people. There are two main systems for this sharing of power between the different administrative levels of a government.

Unitary system
The national, or central, government in a unitary system holds all or most of the power. This central government shares power with its support network of local authorities. One example is the government in Hungary.

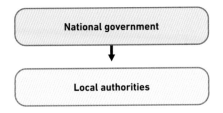

Federal system
Power is shared in a federal system, such as the one in the US. The national government and state governments are responsible for different policies and, in some places, join forces to oversee the work of local authorities.

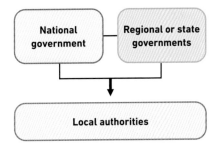

The economy

Every time you buy something or use a service, you contribute to the economy. Citizens also play a part in the economy by producing or distributing these goods and services.

What is an economy?

An economy is a system that involves the production, distribution, and consumption of goods and services. All of these have one thing in common—money. Money is exchanged for goods and services on a daily basis in shops and restaurants and on public transportation. Goods are physical things that can be bought and sold, while services are helpful actions that people provide for others, such as banking and retail. Agriculture produces farmed goods, while manufacturing makes mass-produced goods.

Old and new economies

The economies of some countries that became industrialized earlier now generally focus on services, while newer economies are usually more focused on manufacturing. Since the Industrial Revolution, the manufacturing of factory goods has become an ever-quicker and more efficient process.

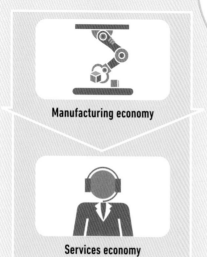

Manufacturing economy

Services economy

Retail
The sale of goods and services via shops and online is a major part of the economy.

Agriculture
Agriculture provides employment and income for many people and food for everyone.

Transportation
An economy is kept moving by a transportation system that takes people around and delivers goods.

Mining
The process of extracting natural, valuable resources from the ground helps the economy.

Fishing
The fishing industry relies on catching and selling fish stocks to markets and restaurants.

Money
Money lies at the heart of every economy.

Education and training
More education may mean more citizens who are likely to be successful in the economy.

Government
Each national government manages goods and services, oversees the exchange of money, and plans for growth.

Types of economy

There are different economies in the world, depending on the political system of the country. Goods and services are essential to all, and in a capitalist economy, they are meant to be based on supply and demand in the market. Most countries adopt one of the following economic systems or use a combination of two. Regardless of the type, there are often problems in all economies, such as inequality, unemployment, and national debt.

Capitalist economy

Citizens can own wealth and property, ideally without government involvement. In reality, governments do get involved, making most of these economies mixed.

Socialist economy

Production and distribution are owned by the public, but private ownership of property is allowed. Profits are used for the benefit of all, and there is equality of opportunity.

Communist economy

The government has complete control of all sectors of the economy. It owns everything on behalf of the people and is meant to share the wealth equally.

Mixed economy

A mixed economy takes ideas from both capitalism and socialism. The government owns and runs some industries, but the rest are privately owned by individuals.

Banking

Loans and investments from banks are necessary to fund new companies, both large and small.

Research

Research results in new, cost-effective, and useful goods, such as medicines.

Manufacturing

An increase in manufacturing creates more jobs and salable goods, thereby helping the economy.

How strong is an economy?

The government monitors and measures the performance of the economy by studying surveys of individuals, businesses, and government departments. Important factors to consider are inflation, growth, and employment. A booming economy checks all three boxes, with soaring profits, rapid expansion, and many employment opportunities.

Inflation

When the prices of goods and services rise year after year, people are able to buy less with the same amount of money. This is called inflation.

Growth

The Gross Domestic Product (GDP), or growth rate, is measured by the total value of the goods and services produced within a country in a single year.

Employment

A healthy economy is one where people who want a job can get one. The proportion of the population out of work reflects the state of the economy.

Why do we pay taxes?

A government needs money to run, and much of this money comes from taxing its citizens. Paying taxes is one way for citizens to contribute to help their country.

Collecting taxes

Taxes are an amount of money paid by each citizen of a country to the government. They are meant to help pay for essential public services that keep society running and support people. The amount of tax that people pay is set by the government, and the money is collected in different ways. Some taxes are collected by the central or national government, while others are taken at a state or local level. It is a citizen's responsibility to pay their taxes on time. It is required by law, and the government can issue fines or prison sentences to punish citizens who do not pay.

Tax havens
Countries that have a low tax rate are sometimes called "tax havens." Some international businesses set up their head offices in these countries in order to avoid paying larger amounts of tax in their home countries.

Goods and services
In some places, shoppers pay a sales tax on items they purchase. It is already included in the item's price. Retailers collect this money and give it to the government.

Income
All working citizens pay a percentage of their earnings directly to the government. The amount each person pays is written on their pay stub.

Property and land
Property and land owners must pay a tax for their homes. The amount of tax paid usually depends on the value of the property.

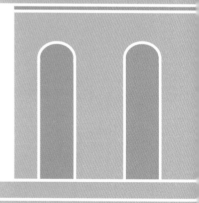

G O V E R

Spending taxes

The government uses the revenue from taxes in different ways—local taxes, for instance, may pay for libraries and schools, while the military is paid for by the central or national government.

Tax systems

In a progressive tax system, wealthy people are meant to pay a higher tax rate on the basis that they can afford to give more without being financially disadvantaged. The opposite is true in a regressive tax system, in which those with a lower income are meant to pay a higher tax rate. These taxes should then be reinvested in services, education, and healthcare to help lower earners. There are also countries in which everyone pays the same tax rate.

Military
Taxes are spent on the training and salaries of military personnel as well as facilities and equipment for the armed forces.

Education and healthcare
Tax revenue pays for public schools, colleges, and universities and partly funds government hospitals and nursing homes in many countries.

Law and order
The government uses money from taxes to pay for the police force and other law enforcement agencies, which protect the country and its citizens.

M E N T

Social welfare
People in need are given financial assistance, benefits, and grants, which are partly paid for by taxes.

Infrastructure
Taxpayers' money is used to help construct buildings, bridges, roads, railways, and sewers. These are costly to build and maintain.

Laws of the land

Every country needs laws. These are the rules that set out how the government should function and how the citizens should behave. Laws protect people and help the government maintain order.

Why we need laws

Every democracy is guided by a set of laws in a constitution. Laws are necessary to make sure citizens' rights are recognized and to guarantee their safety. Criminal law in particular is designed to punish offenders, prevent harm to others, and deter people from committing crimes.

Equality in law

Everyone should be equal under the law and treated impartially without any bias. This idea is represented by a balanced scale, which is also a symbol for justice. In truth, many people from marginalized groups suffer injustice under the law.

How are new laws made?

As well as enforcing existing laws, governments can make new laws. Each planned law is first presented by the government in the legislature, where it is examined and debated. If it is agreed upon, then it is passed by the legislature and then signed into a new law by the executive branch of the government. In some democracies, such as the US, the judiciary can strike down a law that it believes does not follow the constitution.

Types of law

Laws can be of two kinds—public and private. Public laws deal with the functioning of the government and define the rights and responsibilities of citizens. Private laws govern society, overseeing relationships between individuals or between individuals and private organizations.

Public law

Constitutional law
This type relates to the basic rights of every citizen and the rights and powers of the different branches of the government.

Administrative law
These laws manage the daily workings of the government and ensure its actions are in the public interest, such as decisions about taxes.

Criminal law
This type deals with crimes and bringing guilty citizens to justice in courts of law.

Private law

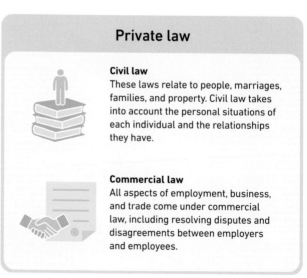

Civil law
These laws relate to people, marriages, families, and property. Civil law takes into account the personal situations of each individual and the relationships they have.

Commercial law
All aspects of employment, business, and trade come under commercial law, including resolving disputes and disagreements between employers and employees.

Enforcing the law

The laws of a country are enforced by different governmental bodies and agencies. These agencies identify, investigate, and capture those who break the law.

Police
This local body maintains law and order in villages, towns, cities, and states.

Federal agencies
These agencies detect, investigate, and prevent crimes across a country or at its borders.

Military
National armed forces protect a nation during conflicts and natural or human-made disasters.

International Court of Justice

This international court deals with international laws that different countries have agreed to follow and solves disputes between countries. It is made up of judges from around the world and was set up in 1945.

The role of courts

The legal system centers around courts of law set up to protect the freedom of citizens and deliver justice fairly and impartially. A court hears all arguments and examines the evidence in detail to establish the facts of a case before a final verdict is given and a sentence is pronounced.

A fair trial
A person accused of a crime has the right to a fair and unbiased trial. Depending on the country, for a criminal case, a judge or a jury is meant to listen impartially to both sides of a case before giving a verdict.

The jury system
In some countries, a group of citizens called a jury sits through a trial to consider the evidence presented in a court. The jury's verdict follows, and a judge gives a sentence based on it.

Punishments
The guilty person may face punishments, such as financial penalties, community service, the temporary loss of some rights, and prison. Rehabilitation may be offered alongside prison sentences to help people rejoin society.

A citizen's rights

Although some people in power may not always agree, all citizens are entitled to equal legal rights, including support from the police and access to courts of law. When a citizen is accused of a crime, they should be presumed innocent until proven guilty, so no assumptions are to be made by those involved in the case before all the evidence is heard. In most cases, a citizen has the right to defend themselves, the right to have a public defender if they cannot afford a lawyer, the right to be given a fair trial, and the right to be in court for the trial.

Seeking help
Citizens accused of crimes can seek the help of a legal counselor or lawyer. These experts on the law are there to give advice, assistance, and information without making any judgments about their clients.

Healthcare

One of the responsibilities of the government is to ensure that citizens lead healthy lives. It monitors and maintains healthcare systems and provides health services on its own or through private organizations.

The government's role

When it comes to healthcare, the government has many tasks to do—from making policies and encouraging people to adopt healthier lifestyles to providing resources for healthcare workers and keeping a check on dangerous diseases. Different governments focus on different areas.

Creating awareness
The government educates citizens about healthy lifestyle choices, hygiene, and the importance of nutrition. In cases of disease outbreaks, it funds large-scale campaigns to create awareness and support the public during the crisis.

Dealing with diseases
The government manages the detection and prevention of infectious diseases—this is particularly important in times of outbreaks that affect the entire population. Medical research, nationwide testing, and vaccination programs that help control diseases are funded by the government.

Maintaining healthcare systems
Hospitals, medical colleges, and training facilities are all essential for keeping the population healthy. Governments either fund the development and maintenance of these institutions or share this responsibility with private organizations.

What is the citizen's responsibility?

Governments and doctors can only do so much. Citizens themselves can also take responsibility for their own well-being by maintaining a healthy lifestyle, being aware of how to access medical care, and following public health advice. In 2020, the World Health Organization (WHO)—an agency of the UN responsible for international public health—called on all citizens to take on more responsibility for staying fit and healthy to reduce the pressure on public health services.

Look after yourself
Citizens should attend medical appointments regularly to keep track of their health.

BE INFORMED

COVID-19 Pandemic

A new disease called COVID-19 spread across the world in 2020, leading to a pandemic. Governments tried to contain the outbreak by using measures such as nationwide lockdowns, social distancing, mandatory mask wearing, handwashing, and large-scale testing.

The healthcare experience

The experience of healthcare varies between countries. Some governments provide free health services to their citizens, while others leave this to private organizations, making it costly for those with medical needs. Expensive basic healthcare makes it difficult for everyone to afford it.

> I envision a world in which everyone can live healthy.
> **Dr. T. A. Ghebreyesus**
> (WHO director-general), 2016

Education

By giving citizens opportunities to build their knowledge and skills, the government can help empower people to succeed in life and contribute to their community and the world.

Education for all

Depending on your age and interests, there are different places where you can learn and improve your skills. Some of these institutions are just for children and young people, while others allow adults to go back to learning once they are older too. Governments are expected to provide education to all citizens.

Schools
Students learn a range of subjects at school, which prepares them for further education.

Higher education
In college, students can study a subject in depth to help their careers.

Apprenticeships
On-the-job training in a specific trade helps build a skilled workforce.

Special programs
Training and learning programs can be adapted for people of all ages or abilities.

Government actions

Governments have a lot of work to do in order to provide all of their citizens with a high-quality education. Their main task is choosing how to spend their education budget (the amount of money the government has available to spend just on education). This budget could be spent on training teachers, providing books or technology to schools, and taking care of or building new places for schools, colleges, and universities to use.

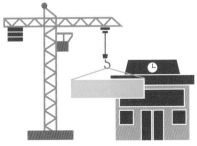

Equity in education
In many countries, not all citizens have access to education. Governments should try to give everyone the same opportunities and help those who have learning difficulties.

Support for teachers
In many countries, the government helps train teachers. It may also offer financial support and classroom resources to teachers to ensure they can do their jobs well.

Developing infrastructure
Governments may be involved in the construction and maintenance of buildings for schools, colleges, and universities to ensure they are safe for students and well equipped.

Challenges to education

In some countries, schools do not have sufficient funding to provide enough teachers, books, and other resources for students to use. This lack of money available for spending on education can lead to unequipped classrooms, classrooms with too many students for one teacher to look after, or a lack of educational opportunities in remote or rural areas. These problems can cause students' education to suffer.

Education is the most powerful weapon which you can use to change the world.
Nelson Mandela (former South African president), Boston, MA, 1990

Resource champions

CHANGE MAKERS: FOOD AND WATER

We may take clean drinking water and nutritious food for granted, but millions of people around the world still do not have access to these basic essentials. Sharing an ambition to make the world a fairer place, many young people from different countries are trying hard to make sure that everyone has access to clean water and healthy food to eat.

Autumn Peltier

Canadian teenager Autumn Peltier, a member of the indigenous Wiikwemkoong First Nation, is fighting for indigenous communities to have access to clean drinking water. Autumn has brought international attention to the rights of indigenous people to water resources on their lands and how these resources are damaged by oil pipelines.

Joshua Williams

In 2005, five-year-old American Joshua Williams was deeply moved by a television commercial about children starving around the world and decided to dedicate his life to fighting hunger. His foundation, Joshua's Heart Foundation, is committed to ending world hunger. Run by young people, the organization provides basic food items to help those in need.

BE INFORMED

Flint water crisis

From 2014 to 2019, the city of Flint, Michigan, suffered a public health crisis when the city's drinking water supply was contaminated with lead, a toxic metal. In 2015, a study conducted by pediatrician Dr. Mona Hanna-Atisha revealed that children in Flint had been exposed to dangerously high levels of lead. Her findings helped the government take measures to resolve the crisis.

Sophie Healy-Thow

Sophie Healy-Thow is a joint winner of the 2014 Google Science Prize for showing how bacteria can help crops grow faster, which is one way to combat food shortages. This Irish campaigner is an advocate for access to food in rural places. People living in these places, which are far from towns and cities, may have lower incomes and limited transportation options, which can make it harder for them to buy food. Sophie also works with organizations that help empower and support farmers and rural women in many countries. One of these organizations is the Scaling Up Nutrition Movement, which aims to end world hunger and malnutrition by bringing together doctors, scientists, and donors from around the world to work on the problem together.

Maya Terro carries meals for distribution.

Maya Terro

Maya Terro

To help feed the hungry in her country, Lebanese Maya Terro set up a volunteer-driven and community-based organization called FoodBlessed in 2012. The organization also tackles food waste by recovering surplus and unsalable food from supermarkets, restaurants, and catering agencies. This food is then distributed to those in need across Lebanon, including Syrian refugees. By 2021, FoodBlessed had given out more than 1,300,000 free meals and had recovered more than 1,102,311 tons of food waste.

Maureen Muketha

Ending malnutrition in her country of Kenya is important for nutritionist Maureen Muketha. Through her organization Tule Vyema, she helps people make healthier meals. She also provides instructions on sack farming, which uses bags of soil and scraps of sacks to grow essential crops.

Georgie Badiel

In 2015, Georgie Badiel established an organization to bring clean water to thousands in her country of Burkina Faso. This organization has helped communities by building and restoring wells and training local communities to maintain wells. Its work has meant that many people no longer have to travel great distances for water.

Political representation

For all citizens to have the chance of being represented in politics, there must be people in positions of power with a similar background to them. Having representatives from all groups should mean that the voices of all people are better heard and considered when the government makes decisions that affect them.

Representation matters

In a democracy, citizens of all genders, sexual identities, races, ethnicities, religions, classes, ages, and abilities have the right to vote for their representatives in government. Elected representatives can then speak on behalf of the people who voted them to power. Ensuring that elected politicians truly represent all groups of citizens means that every person benefits from public policies and that no one is overlooked because of reasons related to their identity.

The importance of diversity
Balanced representation in government means that a diverse set of citizens brings different views to the table. This creates systems that help everyone, rather than the favored few. Although this is far from being achieved in many countries, things are slowly beginning to change.

Who's affected by a lack of representation?

Unfortunately, some sections of society are neglected or discriminated against in the policy-making process, often because there is no one in power who shares their concerns. These groups often struggle for equality, respect, and civil rights because they may be considered unimportant by those in power. Without political representation, the issues these citizens face may be unfairly overlooked by leaders in government, and these people may end up without support or resources.

The only way we'll get freedom... is to identify...with every oppressed people in the world.
Malcolm X (Black civil rights leader), US, 1964

Race
People from certain races and ethnic groups may not be properly represented. Their specific concerns, including discrimination and unfair treatment, may not be heard.

LGBTQ+
People have been discriminated against because of their sexual or gender identities. Members of the LGBTQ+ community often struggle to be represented.

Women
All through history, women have not had as many opportunities to participate in politics as men. Having women in positions of power can help improve gender equality across society.

Indigenous people
The concerns of indigenous people (people native to a region) are often overlooked by governments. Historically, these people have been oppressed by governments or foreign powers.

A more equal future

Although political systems around the world are still not as fair as they could be, progress is slowly being made. To create a fair political system, which includes and represents all groups of people in a country, there are many actions that citizens and governments can take. The ultimate goal is equal representation, where everyone feels their views are heard and respected.

GET INVOLVED

Know your history

Throughout history, many marginalized groups have suffered and fought against discrimination. Reading about history can help you find out which groups of people have been discriminated against and what types of discrimination still occur today.

Raising awareness
Citizens can try to raise awareness of the lack of diversity in government with petitions, publicity, and protests so that more people are aware of the problem. This may encourage those in power to work to change the situation.

Inclusive policies
Governments can promote inclusion at the workplace—for instance, by introducing anti-discrimination policies that stop organizations from denying jobs to people from marginalized groups.

Special committees
Forming new committees made up of people from marginalized groups is a powerful way to ensure that their voices are heard and acknowledged by the government when making decisions about public policy.

Reservations in public office
In some countries, such as India, some roles in government are reserved for candidates from marginalized groups. This approach has been criticized by those who would prefer the selection of candidates to be based only on qualifications.

The fight for Waorani land

CASE STUDY: THE RIGHTS OF INDIGENOUS PEOPLE

The indigenous people of the Waorani Nation live in Ecuador's Amazon Rain Forest. In 2019, they took the Ecuadorian government to court for trying to use a large part of their land for oil drilling without their consent.

16

The number of oil blocks, covering more than 6.2 million acres of land, that the government planned to give out.

340,000+

The number of signatures received from supporters of the Waorani people's digital campaign.

499,153 acres

The area of Waorani land now protected from oil drilling.

What happened?

The Waorani Nation are an indigenous people who live as hunter-gatherers in the Amazon Rain Forest. Their land was threatened when the Ecuadorian government planned to let oil companies use large parts of it to extract oil without permission from the Waorani people. Waorani leader Nemonte Nenquimo (center) filed a lawsuit against the government to halt its plans. The Waorani people organized marches, songs and dances, and a digital campaign, which received a lot of international support.

On April 26, 2019, a court in the city of Puyo, Ecuador, ruled in favor of the Waorani people, confirming their right to their land and protecting it from oil drilling.

Why it happened?

With debts to pay off, the Ecuadorian government planned to generate money by letting foreign companies use land in the Amazon Rain Forest for extracting oil. In doing so, the government failed to consider the interests of indigenous people in the rain forest, such as the Waorani Nation.

Land at stake

Waorani villages are located across their homelands in the Amazon Rain Forest. The Waorani people are dependent on the forests and its rivers for shelter, food, and water.

The response

With help from nonprofit organizations, the Waorani people created and shared digital maps that combined modern technology with their knowledge of the rain forest to show all the places that are important to them and reveal the plant and animal diversity of their region. Support poured in from around the world.

Celebrating victory

Nemonte Nenquimo and other Waorani people marched in celebration through the streets in the city of Puyo after they won.

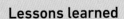

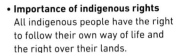

Lessons learned 🔍

- **Importance of indigenous rights**
  All indigenous people have the right to follow their own way of life and the right over their lands.

- **Setting a legal example**
  The court ruling guaranteed the rights of the Waorani people and provided a legal example for other indigenous groups in the Amazon Rain Forest of Ecuador to follow.

- **Protecting the environment**
  The Waorani victory shows how communities can come together to successfully prevent damage from being done to the environment.

GET INVOLVED

Find out more

Indigenous communities are groups of culturally and ethnically distinct people who are native to a particular region of the world. These communities face different types of discrimination and may have to struggle for basic rights. You may have even heard of indigenous people in your own country who are facing these problems. Do some research online or in your local library to find out more about indigenous people around the world, their histories, their rights, and the problems they face.

Recognizing wrongs

All around the world, there are groups of people who have suffered due to the wrongful actions of rulers or governments. Some of these injustices still continue today, and even those that happened in the past still affect people in the present.

A troubled world

The past is full of wrongs, from some nations violently colonizing different parts of the world to some brutal governments displacing and killing millions of their own people. Wars, terrorism (violence against citizens by an individual or a group), and genocide (killing of a large group of people) still happen today. Other acts of injustice that are thought by many to be confined to history continue to have real-world consequences, such as racism in the US, which has its roots in 19th century slavery and still shapes lots of hate and discrimination felt by many Black Americans today. The injustices explained here have happened many times over and are just some examples in a regrettably long list of wrongs.

Suppression
Ruthless governments have often suppressed and controlled populations by cruel means, including forced imprisonment of groups of citizens in labor camps, resulting in the deaths of millions.

Segregation
Some countries have a history of segregation, and this practice of keeping people separate based on race, ethnicity, or nationality continues in some nations today.

Slavery and forced labor
Over the course of history, many powerful rulers and empires have enslaved hundreds of thousands of people, forcing them to work for their own gain while enduring cruelty.

Looting
Many colonists stole treasures from other cultures and communities. Valuable artifacts were often seized and sent to their own nations to be displayed in museums or to be sold off.

Acknowledging errors

It is impossible to bring back lives lost or to rewrite history to undo past or present horrors. But we can confront the mistakes made and acknowledge the problems that continue. These are just some of the reasons why we should do so.

The past informs the present
Although colonialism and atrocities such as the Holocaust seem a long time ago, the groups of people affected, such as the Jewish people, still face discrimination as a result of the prejudice and hatred first stirred up in the past.

Learning from our mistakes
Some countries are trying to learn from their mistakes. For example, in 1988, the US apologized to the Japanese-Americans they unlawfully imprisoned during World War II.

BE INFORMED

Colonialism

Colonialism is the action of one country taking over another by seizing control of the land and dominating the people. While ancient empires also set up colonies, it was during the 18th and 19th centuries that many European powers colonized large parts of Asia, Africa, South America, and North America to expand their empires.

Diminishing cultures

Oppressive regimes can destroy physical things, such as homes and religious buildings, but also parts of people's cultural identities, such as languages, traditions, and livelihoods.

Massacres

Oppressive forces like colonizers or brutal governments often treat large groups of people with cruelty. Millions have been killed in group massacres.

Accountability

The leaders of some countries are trying to make amends by recognizing the harm that was caused, apologizing for it, and taking positive actions. Their methods of making up for the past can take many different forms.

Compensations

Some countries have offered to pay money to those affected by past wrongs.

Museums

Many nations now have museums documenting their past and remembering people who have died.

Memorials and monuments

Monuments dedicated to community heroes help highlight their contributions.

Days of remembrance

Annual memorial days help commemorate lives lost to genocide or war.

Raising awareness

Campaigns such as the UN's Holocaust Outreach Programme teaches today's generations to learn from the past.

Don't let history repeat itself

By understanding past mistakes, nations can take steps to avoid repeating them. International organizations such as the UN work toward world peace and try to stop war crimes and genocide.

Healing our world

Engaging with stories from the past and collectively moving forward can make a better present. Belgium is starting to face up to its colonial past and educate people about the atrocities carried out in what is now the Democratic Republic of Congo.

On the move

Migration is people moving from one place to another. Immigration means moving to another country to live there, while emigration means leaving your country to move somewhere else.

Why do people migrate?

There are many reasons why people move—while work opportunities and a better life may attract people to a different place, economic hardships and conflicts at home may push them away from their own country. With the effects of climate change being felt globally, many people are also being forced to migrate away from natural disasters, such as floods and droughts.

Migration is an expression of the human aspiration for dignity, safety, and a better future.

Ban Ki-moon (former UN secretary-general), 2013

Terms to know	Definitions
Migration	People leaving one place for another. This movement can be within a region or a country or across countries—sometimes in an emergency.
Immigration	People moving into a new country with the intention of settling there. They are called immigrants.
Emigration	People leaving their country with the intention of settling in a different country.
Voluntary migration	People choosing to move from one place to another for personal reasons, such as better work opportunities.
Forced migration	People being displaced from their region or country due to reasons beyond their control, including war, genocides, persecution, or natural disasters.
Asylum seekers	People who are forced to migrate from their country and seek refuge or safety in another country.
Refugees	Asylum seekers who have been granted refuge or safety in a country other than their own, where they are not considered citizens.
Stateless people	People who do not have citizenship in any country.

Migration
People migrate for different reasons at different points in their lives, alone or with their families. They might stay in their new place permanently or return home after a while.

Care for one another

Moving to a new country under any circumstances is challenging, but for people who are forced to flee their homes in an emergency, it is even more difficult. While we often look to governments to help refugees settle in, every citizen can play a part. Start by researching organizations that work to welcome and support refugees in your area or nearby. You may be able to participate in awareness campaigns or fundraisers.

The challenges of moving

Relocating to a new place is challenging for the people moving as well as for the communities they hope to join. While immigration can make societies more multicultural, not everyone sees it that way. Some may find it difficult to accept the arrival of new people into their communities, due to the prejudices they might hold about immigrants or concerns they have about sharing resources. Having an awareness of why people might move regions or countries in search of a better life and the challenges they face in doing so can create empathy and greater understanding between people.

Cultural differences
Different traditions, religious beliefs, and food preferences can make people feel cut-off from new communities.

Language barrier
People often struggle to communicate with others in a new country if they are unfamiliar with the local language.

Lack of social connections
People may feel lonely in their new surroundings if they are far from their family and friends.

Education
Schools and colleges may have different systems, which can interrupt a young person's education.

Employment
Although many people want to work in their new destinations, employment is not always guaranteed.

Health and well-being
Traveling to a new country and adapting to its climate and culture can take a toll on a person's physical and mental health.

Discrimination
People may encounter poor treatment from others who have stereotypical ideas about immigrants.

Housing
It can take time for people moving to a new place to find suitable housing where they feel safe and secure.

The Rohingya crisis

CASE STUDY: FORCED MIGRATION

For decades, the Rohingya people have faced discrimination in Myanmar. Tensions worsened in 2017, when the Myanmar government began a violent military operation that left hundreds of thousands of Rohingya people with no option but to flee.

GET INVOLVED
Find out more

Read up on the Rohingya people and the reasons why they are being persecuted. You may also be interested to find out about other examples in history of groups of people being persecuted for who they are.

No one wants to leave their own home. We've come to Bangladesh only to save our lives. Myanmar is our home.

Sanwara Begum (Rohingya refugee), Kutupalong Refugee Camp, Bangladesh, 2017

What happened?

The Rohingya people, who are mostly Muslim, form an ethnic group who lives in Myanmar, which is mainly Buddhist. Since the 1970s, they have faced discrimination and been persecuted (treated cruelly and unfairly) by the government. Their human rights are not recognized by Myanmar, and they are refused citizenship. Many Rohingya people have had to escape to neighboring countries. The situation worsened in 2017, when the Myanmar military killed thousands of Rohingya people in an act of genocide and forced more than 700,000 to travel to Bangladesh. Many fled on foot to take shelter in makeshift camps, but their future remains uncertain.

Why it happened?

The Rohingya people have been oppressed for more than 50 years in Myanmar due to their religion and ethnicity. The Rohingya crisis peaked in August 2017, when the Myanmar military responded to a militant attack with extreme violence against the Rohingya people. This forced the Rohingya people, fearing for their lives, to flee in huge numbers.

Widespread destruction
In 2017, more than 300 Rohingya villages were burned down in the Myanmar military operation.

Temporary schools
Rohingya children study in makeshift schools set up in the Kutupalong camp in Bangladesh.

The response

Aid for Rohingya refugees has come from around the world. The United Nations (UN) set up camps in Bangladesh and helps run them. Other organizations, such as Save the Children, have given donations and supplies to camps in countries such as Indonesia. The UN has also asked the Myanmar government to stop persecuting the Rohingya people.

Lessons learned

- **Local and global help**
  Urgent help is needed to assist groups of people who are having to rebuild their lives after becoming displaced.

- **International pressure**
  International organizations and other countries should call out governments that discriminate against and persecute minority groups.

- **Long-term solutions**
  As well as providing aid, the international community should try to find long-term solutions by helping refugees settle in another country or safely return to their own.

742,000
The number of Rohingya refugees who have arrived in Bangladesh since 2017.

600,000
The number of Rohingya people at the world's largest refugee camp in Kutupalong, Bangladesh.

354
The number of Rohingya villages destroyed, partially or completely, in 2017.

International law

When different countries agree on common rules that govern how they interact with each other, these rules become legally recognized international laws. They ensure that all countries are treated fairly and that citizens across the world share the same basic human rights.

SEE ALSO

⟨ 18–19 Are we global citizens?

⟨ 50–51 Celebrating differences

⟨ 68–69 What is a government?

⟨ 74–75 Laws of the land

⟨ 86–87 On the move

⟨ 88–89 The Rohingya crisis

Rights champions 92–93 **⟩**

Working together

Nations working together form the basis of all international law. For centuries, kingdoms and countries built alliances and made agreements to avoid conflict and to allow trade in goods between one another. In 1945, after World War II, a global organization called the United Nations (UN) was formed with the goal of bringing together all the nations of the world. Today, the UN is responsible for overseeing agreements between different nations about human rights and a variety of other issues, from the economy to the environment. Formal agreements between countries are called international treaties, which are registered with the UN before becoming law. Beyond the UN, there are also other international organizations that oversee relations between countries.

United Nations (UN)

European Union (EU)

Association of Southeast Asian Nations (ASEAN)

International organizations
Many organizations have lots of member countries working toward common goals.

Enforcing international law

All countries that sign international treaties or join international organizations are expected to follow the laws that govern these alliances. Most countries welcome these laws, but sometimes agreements between countries are broken. When this happens, another country may send diplomats to help them reach a peaceful solution, impose trade bans, or involve international enforcement agencies to make sure that the rules are followed.

Violations and conflicts
Countries may violate international treaties, such as ones governing border sharing, or disregard human rights. Despite having agreed to peace, there may still be conflict between countries.

Enforcement agencies
The International Court of Justice resolves disputes between countries, while the International Criminal Court puts citizens on trial for crimes against humanity, such as those committed during wars.

GET INVOLVED

The Model United Nations (UN) Program

Each year, thousands of children around the world learn more about how the real United Nations (UN) works by taking part in the Model UN Program, which is run in the same way. It helps students learn how the UN operates through talks, debates, and workshops. You may be able to join a school team and participate in Model UN to learn more about international relations. Check to find out whether your school participates!

Universal human rights

Universal human rights are the fundamental things that every human being should be morally and legally entitled to. In 1948, the UN established the Universal Declaration of Human Rights (UDHR). These are the basic human rights that every individual should be able to expect, regardless of their age, physical ability, race, ethnicity, gender, sexual identity, religion, or nationality. Although most countries have adopted the UDHR, sadly, many people are still denied their human rights.

Right to self-determination
Everyone has the right to choose their own path in life.

Right to a nationality
No one can be suddenly denied, or stopped from changing, their nationality.

Right to freedom of movement
Everyone has a right to move around within national borders and leave a country to return to their own.

Right to equality
All human beings are born free and equal in dignity and rights.

Right to justice
Every person is equal before the law and is entitled to equal protection without any discrimination.

Right to fair treatment before the law
Everyone is entitled to a fair public hearing by an independent and impartial court.

Right to take part in government
All members of a society should be free to take part in government activities directly or through their representatives.

Right to protest
Everyone has the freedom to assemble peacefully in order to protest.

Right to social security
Everyone should have enough money and be guaranteed safety in circumstances beyond their control, such as sickness or old age.

Right to asylum
Everyone has the right to seek asylum or safety in other countries in case of persecution.

Freedom of thought and expression
Everyone can have opinions as well as seek, receive, and give ideas without interference.

Right to education
Everyone is entitled to an education. Primary education should ideally be free and mandatory.

Right to employment and equal pay
Everyone should have free choice of employment, fair and favorable working conditions, and equal pay for equal work.

Right to adequate standards of living
Everyone is entitled to a standard of living that is adequate for their good health and well-being.

Right to privacy
Everyone has a right to a private life free of unnecessary interference.

Right to own property
Everyone has the right to own property alone as well as in association with others.

Right to marry
Everyone of legal age has the right to marry without limitation of race, ethnicity, nationality, or religion.

Right to rest and relaxation
Everyone has the right to rest and relaxation, reasonable limits on working hours, and time off.

Murad with
her Nobel
Peace Prize

Nadia Murad

Nadia Murad is one of the Yazidi people, an
ethnic and religious minority group from Iraq.
In 2014, an Islamic extremist group called the
Islamic State (ISIS) attacked her village, killing
600 men and kidnapping many young women,
including Nadia. This was part of a brutal
operation by ISIS to remove all the Yazidi
people from the country. Nadia suffered abuse
for three months before escaping. She began
sharing her experiences and those of others
and is now a champion for women and
children who have endured violence, abuse,
and human trafficking. She won the Nobel
Peace Prize in 2018 for her work.

> We must work toward a
> future in which the entire
> world, not just the Yezidis,
> say "never again."
>
> **Nadia Murad**, UN interview, 2019

Rights champions

CHANGE MAKERS: HUMAN RIGHTS

Discrimination can lead to abuse, violence, and the denial of people's basic human rights. But many young champions all over the world are pushing back and fighting to protect the safety and human rights of society's most vulnerable people.

Taji Chesimet

Following the killing of 17-year-old Quanice Hayes by the police in 2017, Taji Chesimet co-founded an organization to promote racial equality and justice in Portland, Oregon. Known as Raising Justice, this youth-backed organization aims to reduce systemic racism and make it safer for young Black people to be in public. It has offered training on youth relations to more than 1,000 officers in the city's police bureau.

Ikponwosa Ero

Nigerian lawyer Ikponwosa Ero specializes in developing policies that can help people with albinism. This is a condition where the skin, hair, or eyes lack any pigment or color. Ikponwosa has albinism herself and has worked for years to stop violent, discriminatory attacks on people with albinism all over the world. In 2015, she started working with the UN to ensure that people with albinism are not denied their human rights.

Harry Myo Lin

As a Muslim in the mainly Buddhist country of Myanmar, Harry Myo Lin fights for peace and religious tolerance in his country. When riots broke out between Buddhists and Muslims in the Rakhine state in 2012, he used social media to bring people of different faiths together and fight hate speech. He also runs courses on bringing about peaceful solutions to conflict.

BE INFORMED

UNHCR

The UNHCR, the UN's refugee agency, is an organization that works to protect and help people who have been forcibly displaced from their homes, such as refugees, asylum seekers, and stateless people. With a global network of refugee camps, the UNHCR provides displaced individuals and groups with food, shelter, and medical help. It also supports them with adapting to life in their new countries, with resettling into a different country if needed, or with returning to their country of origin, if possible.

Nidhi Goyal

The work done by this disabled feminist has highlighted the sexual violence faced by disabled girls and women in India and their struggles for justice. Nidhi Goyal seeks to improve their lives. She set up the Rising Flame organization in Mumbai to support disabled people, assisted by many human rights and women's rights organizations.

Our environment

RAISING ENVIRONMENTAL AWARENESS AND
TAKING ACTION TO PROTECT OUR PLANET

❝ The climate movement cannot be stopped. We know what we want because it is our future at stake. We need a secure future for ourselves and the coming generations after us. ❞

Vanessa Nakate (Ugandan climate champion),
Voices of Youth, 2020

Our changing world

The world around us is changing because of human activity. Our growing population and the rising demand for resources are affecting animals and plants, the environment, and the climate.

What is the climate crisis?

Throughout the history of our planet, there have been gradual changes to the climate due to natural causes, such as volcanic eruptions. However, human activity in the last 70 years has caused Earth's climate to change rapidly. Levels of heat-trapping gases, such as carbon dioxide, in the atmosphere have risen sharply, causing average temperatures to rise, affecting Earth's climate. Climate change is making life harder for all species on the planet, including humans. This is the climate crisis we face today.

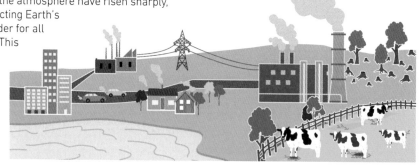

Human activity
Burning fossil fuels, deforestation, and farming are among the main sources of greenhouse gases, such as carbon dioxide and methane, given off by human activity.

What's happening?

The impact of human activity is warming up our planet at an alarming rate. This has triggered a chain of events that affects the atmosphere, the oceans, the land, animals, plants, and humans.

Ocean warming
Rising temperatures result in warmer oceans, causing polar ice sheets to melt. Animals such as polar bears find it harder to hunt and move around.

Rising sea level
Melting polar ice sheets and glaciers cause sea levels to rise. Low-lying coastal areas are at risk of flooding, and smaller islands may go underwater.

Extreme weather
As the climate warms, extreme weather conditions, such as intense wildfires, longer droughts, and powerful storms, are becoming more common.

Habitat loss
As habitats heat up, changing temperatures can make it harder for some species to survive. Some animals may move to cooler regions, which affects food chains.

Reduced food supply
Changing weather patterns and inconsistent rainfall reduce the amount of crops, leading to food shortages. This leads to higher food prices and problems with the food supply.

The decline of nature

Many species are struggling to adapt to climate change. At the same time, they are threatened by habitat loss. Forests, for example, have been increasingly cut down since the 1700s, mainly due to growing demand for wood and for land for growing crops and grazing animals. Many species have been driven to extinction because of deforestation, and many more are at risk of disappearing.

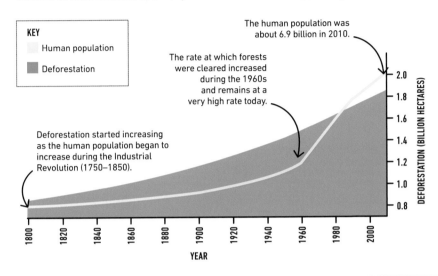

KEY
- Human population
- Deforestation

The human population was about 6.9 billion in 2010.

The rate at which forests were cleared increased during the 1960s and remains at a very high rate today.

Deforestation started increasing as the human population began to increase during the Industrial Revolution (1750–1850).

DEFORESTATION (BILLION HECTARES)

2.0
1.8
1.6
1.4
1.2
1.0
0.8

YEAR: 1800, 1820, 1840, 1860, 1880, 1900, 1920, 1940, 1960, 1980, 2000

Studying climate change

Scientists collect data from satellites, ocean monitoring stations, weather balloons, and weather ships to study climate change. They also take samples from prehistoric ice, rock, ocean sediment, and tree rings to track climate conditions throughout history and predict how the climate will change in the future if greenhouse gas emissions don't decrease.

Changing seasons
Plant growth and the harvesting of crops depend on seasonal cycles staying the same. Changes in these cycles can affect the growth of plants and crops.

Homes and livelihoods at risk
Climate change can destroy homes and livelihoods. Flooding, bush fires, and droughts often force people away from their homes.

Depleting resources

As our population grows and towns and cities spread, greater pressure is put on our planet's limited natural resources. More people means ever-increasing demand for water, food, land, and fossil fuels. Today, the total amount of natural resources being consumed by humans is about 10 times higher than it was in 1900!

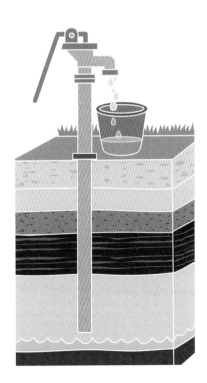

Water crisis
Freshwater reserves (naturally occurring water not from the sea or ocean) are depleting around the world. This is caused by higher temperatures and droughts shrinking rivers and reservoirs as well as by increasing water demand from industries, such as agriculture and food production. Although about 70 percent of Earth is covered in water, humans cannot drink much of that.

Climate champions

CHANGE MAKERS: CLIMATE CHANGE

The voices of these young people are drawing attention to the need for urgent action against global warming and climate change. By spearheading protests, marches, and strikes, these climate campaigners are raising awareness on an unprecedented scale.

Eyal Weintraub

Argentinian climate campaigner Eyal Weintraub organized a protest at the National Congress in Buenos Aires in 2019, calling for action on global warming. He cofounded the organization called *Jóvenes por el Clima Argentina* (Youth for Climate Argentina).

Jamie Margolin

American teenager Jamie Margolin has been a leading voice at climate action rallies in the US since 2017. Her organization, Zero Hour, aims to inform and educate communities around the world about the root causes of the climate crisis and gain support for action against climate change.

Lance Lau Hin-yi

In 2019, despite being just 10 years old, Lance Lau Hin-yi began staging solo protests every Friday morning outside his school in Hong Kong. His goal is to raise awareness about limiting greenhouse gases and cleaning up beaches and to encourage more children to play a part in environmental action.

BE INFORMED

Green New Deal

American Congresswoman Alexandria Ocasio-Cortez set out a new plan for managing climate change in 2019. The Green New Deal called on the US government to reduce the reliance on fossil fuels and increase the use of renewable sources of energy.

The eyes of all future generations are upon you. And if you choose to fail us, I say—we will never forgive you.

Greta Thunberg, UN Climate Action Summit, New York, 2019

Greta Thunberg

Greta Thunberg (bottom center) is one of the most well-known young people speaking out about climate change. In 2018, when she was 15, Greta skipped school to protest outside the Swedish Parliament with a sign stating, "school strike for climate." She has made speeches in front of world leaders, and her work has inspired some of the planet's largest climate strikes, including young people from more than 125 countries.

Vanessa Nakate

Worried by the extreme weather caused by climate change in her country, Uganda, climate campaigner Vanessa Nakate (bottom right) protested alone before attracting other climate champions. She started the Rise Up Movement in 2019 to encourage young people in Africa to take climate action.

The carbon problem

The amount of the element carbon in the atmosphere is determined by a natural cycle. Human activities have altered this cycle, increasing the levels of carbon dramatically.

The greenhouse effect

Earth's atmosphere contains trace gases, such as carbon dioxide and methane, that trap heat like the glass in a greenhouse, making the planet warm enough for life to exist. These are called greenhouse gases. Human activity over the last 70 years has rapidly increased the level of these gases in the atmosphere, enhancing their effect. As they build up, they trap more heat, causing Earth's average temperature to rise. This process is called global warming, and it is the main reason for climate change today.

> We are the first generation to feel the impact of climate change and the last generation that can do something about it.
> **Barack Obama** (former US president), UN Climate Change Summit, 2014

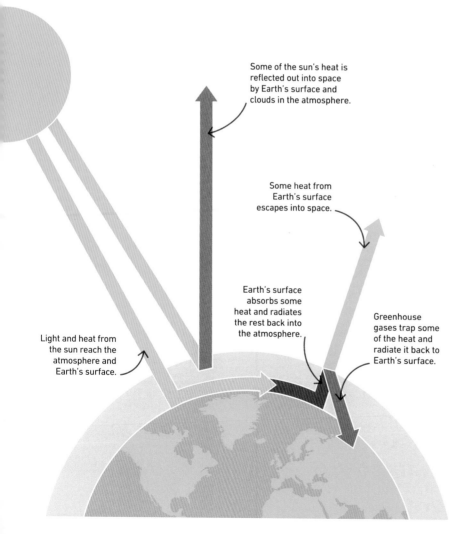

Some of the sun's heat is reflected out into space by Earth's surface and clouds in the atmosphere.

Some heat from Earth's surface escapes into space.

Earth's surface absorbs some heat and radiates the rest back into the atmosphere.

Greenhouse gases trap some of the heat and radiate it back to Earth's surface.

Light and heat from the sun reach the atmosphere and Earth's surface.

Ocean release

Ocean absorption

Farming

Photosynthesis

The carbon cycle

Carbon, which is present in all living things, flows through the air, the ocean, and the ecosystems on land in the form of a gas called CO_2. Natural processes once kept the amount of this greenhouse gas in balance. Volcanic eruptions and respiration in plants and animals release carbon dioxide into the atmosphere, while oceans absorb it, as do plants when making food during a process called photosynthesis. However, human activities in recent times, such as deforestation and emissions from fossil fuels, have tipped the balance in favor of carbon, releasing more carbon dioxide into the atmosphere than natural processes can remove. This gas is the largest contributor to global warming.

KEY

↓ CO_2 removed from the atmosphere

↑ CO_2 added to the atmosphere by natural processes

↑ CO_2 added to the atmosphere by human activity

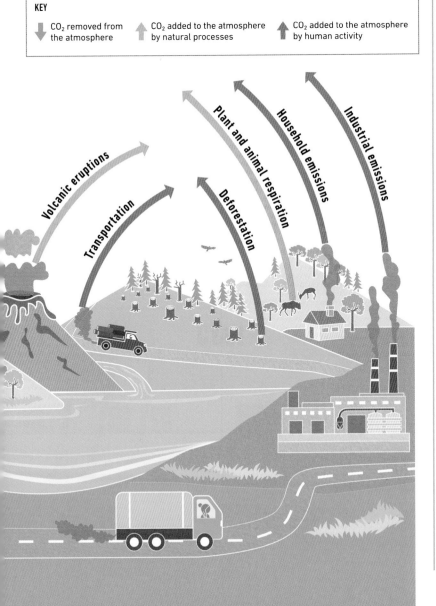

Carbon footprint

A carbon footprint is the total amount of carbon dioxide released by activities carried out by a person, an organization, or a country. For an individual, their daily activities contribute to their carbon footprint. These can include watching TV, for example, which may use electricity that has been produced by burning carbon-releasing fossil fuels.

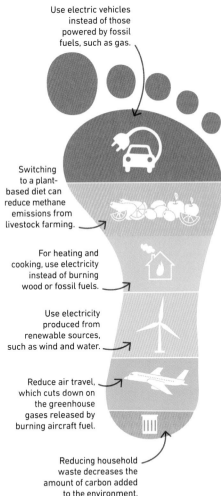

Use electric vehicles instead of those powered by fossil fuels, such as gas.

Switching to a plant-based diet can reduce methane emissions from livestock farming.

For heating and cooking, use electricity instead of burning wood or fossil fuels.

Use electricity produced from renewable sources, such as wind and water.

Reduce air travel, which cuts down on the greenhouse gases released by burning aircraft fuel.

Reducing household waste decreases the amount of carbon added to the environment.

Reducing our carbon footprint
Each country has a carbon footprint. Governments, organizations, and individuals can all contribute toward reducing this footprint.

Pollution

When harmful substances are added to the environment, we call it pollution. Our planet is being polluted at an increasing rate as a result of human activities.

A polluted world

Human actions pollute the air, land, and water. Chemicals and litter dirty the water, while dangerous emissions make the air harmful to breathe and speed up the warming of our planet. As natural habitats are destroyed and societies spread out, the landscape is changed for ever. It can be disheartening to learn about the damage humans have done to the planet, but knowing what the problems are is the first step toward finding the solutions.

Polluting the air
The burning of fossil fuels, such as coal, petroleum, and natural gas, is the main source of air pollution. Thick smoke from factories and power plants mixes with vehicle emissions, producing dense clouds of smog that blanket many cities. As well as causing breathing problems for people, burning these fuels produces greenhouse gases, which accelerate the warming of our planet.

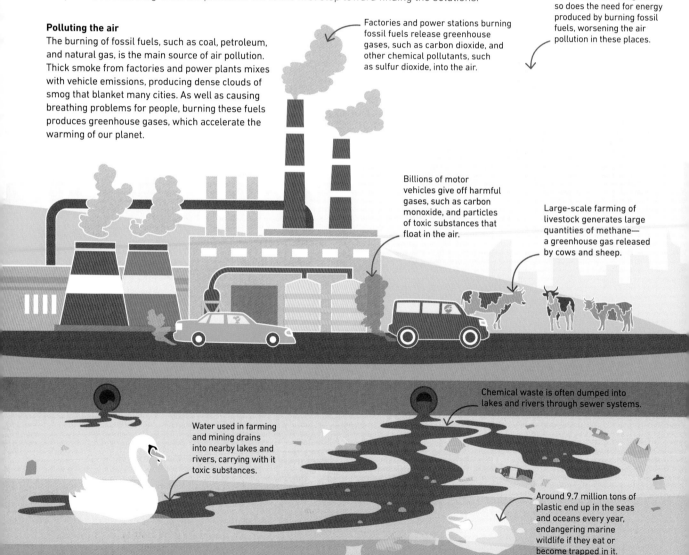

Factories and power stations burning fossil fuels release greenhouse gases, such as carbon dioxide, and other chemical pollutants, such as sulfur dioxide, into the air.

As towns and cities grow, so does the need for energy produced by burning fossil fuels, worsening the air pollution in these places.

Billions of motor vehicles give off harmful gases, such as carbon monoxide, and particles of toxic substances that float in the air.

Large-scale farming of livestock generates large quantities of methane— a greenhouse gas released by cows and sheep.

Chemical waste is often dumped into lakes and rivers through sewer systems.

Water used in farming and mining drains into nearby lakes and rivers, carrying with it toxic substances.

Around 9.7 million tons of plastic end up in the seas and oceans every year, endangering marine wildlife if they eat or become trapped in it.

> Every breath of air we take...comes from the natural world. And if we damage the natural world, we damage ourselves.

Sir David Attenborough (British natural historian), World Economic Forum, Switzerland, 2019

Manage waste

You can reduce pollution by monitoring and managing your own waste. Start by reducing the number of things you buy and purchasing items with less packaging to minimize plastic waste. Separate your household waste into glass, plastic, paper, and food to be recycled in bins and banks.

Degrading the land
If factories don't dispose of their toxic waste carefully, hazardous substances can seep into the soil. This can endanger the ecosystem and cause plants and animals to die. Huge mounds of trash at landfills not only ruin the landscape but are also harmful for people living nearby.

The extraction of natural resources, such as coal or oil, from deep underground involves clearing trees and digging huge holes. These activities can poison the soil and water in the area. Humans may also be at a risk of exposure to dangerous chemicals and gases.

Tons of garbage dumped in landfills every year release harmful substances, such as mercury and lead, that can damage the soil.

Using too many chemicals on crops can kill beneficial microorganisms that live in soil, causing it to lose fertility. Chemicals also harm insects that are essential for the pollination of crops.

Contaminating water
The water in lakes, rivers, seas, and oceans is polluted by toxic substances, such as industrial chemicals, sewage from cities, and litter thrown away by people. These pollutants are deadly for aquatic plants and animals and often contaminate the water we use for our daily activities.

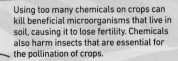

Oil spills from oil tankers float on water and poison marine wildlife.

Plants and animals

As our population grows and our industries and farms expand, the combined impact of our actions affects many plant and animal species, making life much harder, and in some cases impossible, for them.

Why plants and animals matter

Humans are only one species among millions that call Earth home and deserve to thrive on it. Our society has only developed because of the resources offered by Earth's ecosystems and the species living in them. All our oxygen and water is recycled by nature. Oceans and forests absorb huge amounts of carbon dioxide, while all our food comes from animals and plants. Many medicines were developed from substances first found in the wild. As habitats are lost and species become extinct, the natural benefits they provide and that we depend upon are also at risk of being lost.

What are the problems?

Human activity is causing plant and animal species to die out at a rate not seen on Earth since the time the dinosaurs disappeared 66 million years ago. This problem is worsening with the rising demand for resources because of our growing population.

Rising temperatures
The rising temperatures caused by burning fossil fuels are melting polar ice and glaciers, raising sea levels and killing coral reefs.

Deforestation
Rain forests, home to millions of species, are cleared to create farmland to produce food for farm animals, to make plantations for paper, and to grow plants for vegetable oil.

Pollution
Harmful substances produced by human activities contaminate the land, air, and water, which can make habitats impossible for some creatures to continue living in.

Overexploitation
Catching and eating animals such as fish faster than their populations can replenish put the existence of the species at risk.

Extreme weather
Climate change is shifting seasonal patterns and changing natural habitats to the point where some species aren't able to adapt.

Mountain peatland and other wetlands, such as lowland bogs, store supplies of water.

Forests absorb carbon dioxide from the atmosphere.

Wetlands and forests slow the downhill flow of water toward rivers or streams, preventing soil erosion.

Impact of human activities

Many species are endangered as their habitats are damaged and lost, and their numbers are depleted by hunting and overexploitation. Humans are also responsible for introducing "invasive species" in places where they were once not found. These species compete with local plants and animals for food.

Loss of habitats

As habitats are lost due to clearing land for farming and developing urban areas, plants and animals may struggle to find areas in which they can survive.

Extinction of species

The combined pressure of human activities has driven many species close to extinction (dying out).

Food webs disrupted

As plants and animals die out, food chains are affected. The reduced numbers of one species can lead to prey or other predators increasing in number, which makes entire food webs (sets of food chains) imbalanced.

Fewer pollinators

Most land plants depend on insects, such as bees and butterflies, to pollinate their flowers. These insects are threatened by habitat loss.

Scavenging birds such as vultures feed on rotting animal bodies, clearing them from land.

Tracking endangered species

There are international organizations working to monitor the numbers of animal and plant species around the world. The International Union for Conservation of Nature (IUCN) studies the numbers of at-risk species and shows how endangered a particular species is on its Red List.

Not evaluated
This category includes all species that have not yet been assessed by the IUCN.

Data deficient
There are not enough data to assess the risk of extinction for these species, such as the Elliot's storm petrel seabird.

Least concern
Species with thriving numbers, such as the silver fir, are the least likely to become extinct in the near future.

Near threatened
These species, including the maned wolf, are close to being vulnerable in the near future.

Vulnerable
Species such as the reef manta ray are vulnerable and could become endangered unless action is taken.

Endangered
Species at high risk of extinction in the wild, such as the mountain gorilla, are classified as endangered.

Critically endangered
Species such as the Sumatran tiger are at an extremely high risk of extinction in the wild.

Extinct in the wild
The Guam kingfisher is one of many species that exist only in captivity or in areas other than their natural habitats. They are extinct in the wild.

Extinct
These are species with no living members in the world. One example is the West African black rhinoceros.

Levels of danger
The IUCN Red List separates species into nine different categories, depending on the current level of threat to their existence.

> The question is, are we happy to suppose that our grandchildren may never be able to see an elephant except in a picture book?
> **Sir David Attenborough** (British natural historian), 2019

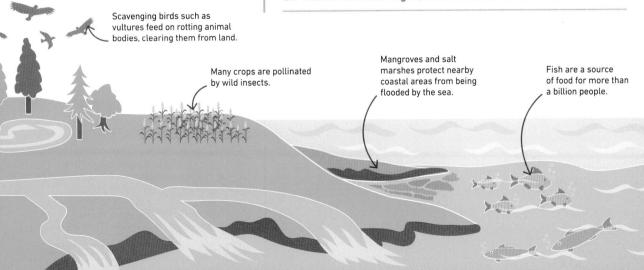

Many crops are pollinated by wild insects.

Mangroves and salt marshes protect nearby coastal areas from being flooded by the sea.

Fish are a source of food for more than a billion people.

Nature champions

CHANGE MAKERS: PLANTS AND ANIMALS

Many young people are trying to protect Earth's animals and save its plants by raising awareness of the issues they face and campaigning for action.

Duncan Jurman

Butterfly enthusiast Duncan Jurman started the environmental project Bring Butterflies Back to raise awareness about declining butterfly populations in his home state of Florida. He teaches young students about how butterflies are important to various ecosystems, and grows nectar-producing plants that help attract more butterflies to the area. Duncan has also raised more than 5,000 butterflies in his butterfly garden over the years.

Thomas Ponce

Since Thomas Ponce decided to become a vegetarian at four years old, his passion for animal rights has continued to develop. As a teenager in the US, Thomas founded the organization Lobby for Animals in 2012. It stands against cruelty to all living beings and encourages people to campaign for an end to the suffering of animals in slaughterhouses, factory farms, and laboratories worldwide.

BE INFORMED

Reteti Elephant Sanctuary

This animal sanctuary in northern Kenya is the result of a community-run conservation movement. It is home to Kenya's second-largest elephant population. The caretakers at Reteti look after orphaned or abandoned elephant calves, with the aim of releasing them into the wild. Local people from Samburu County help in rescuing and treating adult elephants as well.

Aadhiyagai Parameswaran

Indian engineer Aadhiyagai Parameswaran learned about farming from his parents. An organic farming workshop gave him the idea that gathering native seeds would benefit farmers. Over three years, he built up a bank of seeds from the fruits and vegetables of more than 300 plants. He now sells the seeds to farmers at low costs to promote local produce.

Felix Finkbeiner

A class on climate change and the importance of tree-planting inspired nine-year-old Felix Finkbeiner to form Plant-for-the-Planet, an environmental organization that helped plant 100,000 trees in his native Germany within its first year. More than a decade later, with support from the UN, this environmental campaigner has helped plant more than 15 billion trees across 130 countries.

Madison Stewart

Nicknamed "Shark Girl," Australian diver Madison fell in love with sharks at the age of 14 while scuba diving off the Great Barrier Reef. Her disappointment at their declining numbers led her to film people fishing sharks to raise awareness of this growing problem. Madison's documentaries have gained support for shark conservation and protection for the most vulnerable species. At 24, she was recognized as the Australian Geographic Society Young Conservationist of the Year.

Madison Stewart

Impact on humans

Global warming because of climate change is changing our environment in ways that will make it increasingly difficult for humans to live well on Earth. The scale of this problem is now impossible to ignore.

Challenges for all

In the last 170 years, the average global temperature has risen by about 1.8°F (1.0°C). This is a drastic shift that has taken place over a short time, and it's enough to trigger a chain of events that has plunged the world into crisis. As human activity accelerates global warming and climate change, our world is transforming faster than ever, with communities around the world facing many problems.

Heat waves and fires
Some places endure heatwaves as temperatures soar. Long, hot, dry spells can also ignite forest fires, endangering wildlife and destroying homes.

Desertification and droughts
Hotter and drier weather causes droughts and leads to the spread of desert regions as fertile land dries out. This process is called desertification.

Damage to ecosystems
Climate change can lead to particular species of plants and animals dying out or wildlife moving away in search of food. This can destroy entire ecosystems.

Storms
Warmer air rising over the oceans creates storms, which are becoming stronger and more frequent and are lasting longer. Some of the worst examples of extreme weather are brutal hurricanes and cyclones.

Flooding
Rising sea levels pose a threat to coastal cities, low-lying regions, and islands. Unusually heavy rainfall also causes frequent flooding, leading to loss of life and property.

Melting ice and rising sea levels
Rising global temperatures are causing vast ice sheets at the poles to melt. The additional water leads to a rise in sea levels, which can cause flooding. Arctic wildlife, such as polar bears, that depends on ice struggles to survive as their habitat melts away.

Damaged infrastructure
As well as loss of human life, extreme weather can damage infrastructure—including roads, buildings, bridges—or make them unusable. People in these areas may be forced to flee and may find themselves homeless.

Food and water shortages
Floods and droughts affect food production and can lead to food shortages or price hikes that make some items unaffordable. Droughts can also cause water shortages.

No challenge poses a greater threat to future generations than climate change.
Barack Obama (former US president), State of the Union Address, Washington, DC, 2015

Spread of disease
Diseases such as cholera and malaria are more likely to spread in warmer or wetter conditions. If flooding occurs, flood waters can become contaminated by overflowing sewage, spreading diseases.

Crop failure and soil erosion
In extreme weather, crops can fail, reducing the amount of food available for people. Heavy rainfall or dry weather can wash away or dry out soil, leaving it unsuitable for farming.

Climate migration
Flooding, desertification, and rising sea levels may force people to move in search of safer locations as the damaging effects of climate change make it impossible to stay.

Conflict
The growing number of environmental challenges can cause conflict between communities and between neighboring countries, as resources become increasingly scarce.

Fires in Australia

CASE STUDY: CLIMATE CHANGE

Long spells of very hot and dry weather, made more likely by climate change, triggered an outbreak of forest fires in Australia in 2019. The fires raged for months, causing widespread devastation.

42,000 miles^2

The area of land burned. This added to the global problem of forest loss.

What happened?

Fires first broke out in the Australian states of New South Wales and Victoria in September 2019. They burned through forests and bushlands for many months. Emergency helicopters dropped water on the fires, but they still spread at lightning speed.

At least 34 people lost their lives, while many were left homeless. Billions of animals were injured or killed, and wildlife habitats were destroyed. The fires produced a toxic cloud of smoke three times the size of Europe. More carbon dioxide was released by the fires than Australia usually produces in an entire year. It was only after a lot of effort that the fires were finally put out in March 2020.

3,094

The number of homes destroyed. Those left homeless needed temporary shelter.

1.25 billion

The number of animals killed. Nearly 3 billion animals were affected by the fires.

5,185

The Air Quality Index (AQI) level recorded in Canberra due to smoke—50 times more than safe levels.

26 percent

The number of businesses affected. The travel, tourism, and food industries were the worst hit.

Why it happened?

Before the fires, high temperatures and low rainfall caused severe droughts. The conditions made the bush very dry and likely to catch fire from lightning strikes.

113°F
(45°C)

69.8°F
(21°C)

Temperatures in 2019

Lessons learned

- **Monitor forests**
  Forests and bushlands that may easily catch fire should be monitored by the government to detect fires early.

- **Reduce greenhouse gases**
  A reduction in the release of greenhouse gases is required to combat global warming as it worsens natural disasters.

- **Spread climate awareness**
  Talk to family, friends, and classmates to raise awareness of climate change and inform people about what they can do to help stop the problem.

The response

Australia's government declared a national emergency, and thousands of firefighters went to work. Military aid, such as aircraft and troops, was sent in. Support also poured in from across the globe in the form of fundraisers, volunteer firefighters, and donations.

Rescuing wildlife

Rescue teams risked their lives to save animals caught up in the forest fires. This koala was lucky to have escaped.

GET INVOLVED

Preventing fires

Follow the rules while making an open fire if you go out camping, or if you are having a bonfire or cookout in your backyard. Build, monitor, and put out your fire with care and attention. At home, trim shrubs and cut grass regularly if you have a yard. Keep dead leaves from gathering around your home by raking them, and make sure there are no flammable materials nearby.

Living sustainably

The growing human population has put huge pressure on our planet. Together, we need to find ways to live on Earth without using up its limited resources. The goal is to protect the planet and its resources for future generations.

What is sustainability?

Sustainability means meeting our needs for food, energy, health, and housing in ways that allow future generations to meet their needs too. It involves protecting and restoring Earth's forests and oceans, conserving species living in them, and supporting lifestyles and practices that reduce human impact on the environment. Governments and businesses need to consider the environmental impact when creating jobs, running our economies, and meeting the needs of everyone in society.

> The greatest danger to our planet is the belief that someone else will save it.
>
> **Robert Swan** (British explorer), *HuffPost*, 2012

The economy
Not prioritizing profits at the expense of the environment should be a goal for all businesses. They can try to be profitable without overusing natural resources or polluting the environment.

The environment
The natural environment is the source of all our natural resources, which are finite and won't last for ever. Adopting an eco-friendly lifestyle will mean Earth's resources are used at a more sustainable rate.

Society
In a sustainable society, all citizens have access to opportunities and good living standards, without compromising or damaging the environment.

Sustainable development

Sustainability can be achieved by considering the needs of the economy, the environment, and society at the same time. We need to pay equal attention to all three areas, as focusing more on any one of them at the cost of the others is unsustainable.

A need for change

As the population grows, there is greater demand for Earth's natural resources, which are limited. The current rate at which we are consuming them cannot be sustained for ever. In fact, some studies have shown that we have fewer than 50 years to change our behavior before oil and natural gas run out.

BE INFORMED

Gardens by the Bay

The striking, steel "Supertrees" at the Gardens by the Bay in Singapore house more than 700 plant species. These sustainable structures collect rainwater for reuse and generate electricity through solar panels.

Looking to the future

Creating a sustainable world is the only way for human societies to continue to thrive in the future. Living sustainably involves individuals and communities changing their behaviour to be more eco-friendly and governments, businesses, and organizations developing new policies and technologies that don't harm the environment. All of us need to take steps to protect our planet for future generations.

GET INVOLVED

Learn about sustainability

The Internet, books, and documentaries can help you learn more about sustainability and the environment. With friends, discuss small, simple steps you can each take to make your lifestyles more sustainable, such as reducing your waste or buying fewer items. Think about the changes you'd like to see businesses, societies, and governments make too. You could ask a teacher at school to discuss the same topics in your classroom.

Reversing the damage
There are many ways for people to live more sustainably, and while it may take time, it is not impossible to reverse the damage done to the environment.

Sustainable living
Low-emission ways of living, working, and traveling can help combat the climate emergency. Energy-efficient towns and cities of the future will probably use long-lasting, eco-friendly materials and have lots of green spaces.

Zero-waste economies
Zero-waste economies aim to reuse or recycle all items that people have thrown away so that nothing is sent to landfill sites. This preserves Earth's natural resources for longer and reduces pollution created by landfills.

Sustainable farming
Growing food in a sustainable way means avoiding deforestation, reducing farming emissions, not using too much water, and giving soil enough time to replenish its nutrients. We can take care of the land by consuming only what we need.

Restoring ecosystems
By planting more trees and conserving wildlife, we may be able to restore damaged ecosystems. Local conservation efforts can be supported by ecotourism, in which people visit natural habitats without affecting the environment.

Clean and renewable energy
Replacing fossil fuels almost completely with renewable energy, such as solar and wind power, will reduce greenhousega-s emissions. Using electric and hybrid vehicles powered by renewable energy can also reduce emissions.

Environmental policies

Around the world, governments and organizations are introducing new policies to combat the climate crisis and ensure that we use Earth's limited natural resources in a sustainable way.

Global goals

In 2015, the United Nations General Assembly set up new Sustainable Development Goals (SDGs), a set of 17 social and environmental targets to be met by 2030. In total, 193 nations have signed up to support these goals, which aim to create a more fair and equal world where communities and economies prosper while protecting the environment. The goals cover a diverse range of challenges, including providing clean water and sanitation, conserving wildlife, taking action to combat climate change, creating sustainable cities and communities, and producing affordable, clean energy.

BE INFORMED

THE IPCC

The Intergovernmental Panel on Climate Change (IPCC) is a UN body that assesses the impacts of climate change and recommends the actions needed to prevent it from reaching dangerous levels. The IPCC also produces special reports that provide suggestions for governments to prepare well for extreme weather events, such as tornados, floods, and droughts.

International efforts

Countries have started working together to tackle the global climate crisis by signing international treaties pledging to take action to protect the planet. Countries with more developed economies often produce more greenhouse gases. They may need to support countries with less developed economies, as these nations are likely to suffer the worst effects of climate change while having done the least to cause it.

Montreal Protocol
Signed in 1987, this treaty banned chemicals that are harmful to the atmosphere's ozone layer and also cause global warming.

Rio Summit
At the 1992 Earth Summit in Rio de Janeiro, Brazil, the United Nations agreed on new treaties to reduce greenhouse gases.

Kyoto Protocol
This international treaty in 1997 brought together 84 countries with industries and set out targets for reducing greenhouse-gas emissions.

Paris Agreement
The goal of this 2016 agreement, signed by 197 countries, is to limit the increase in global average temperature to well below 3.6°F (2°C).

Countries at work

Individual countries are setting their own targets to combat climate change. Many nations have introduced policies and set up new programs to reduce pollution, restore forests, and make the switch to renewable energy sources.

The United Kingdom
The Climate Change Act of 2008 aims to reduce the UK's greenhouse-gas emissions to net zero by 2050.

Canada
Canada has a tax on using fossil fuels, such as oil, coal, and gas. The tax is based on the amount of greenhouse gases emitted.

China
A road space-rationing policy in Beijing, China, allows only certain vehicles on the roads on weekdays to limit harmful vehicle emissions.

Costa Rica
About 98 percent of Costa Rica's electricity comes from renewable power sources, including water, wind, and the sun.

The Gambia
A project in the Gambia is working to restore 24,710 acres (10,000 hectares) of forests and wildlife parks by planting trees and conserving species of shrubs.

How can businesses contribute?

Businesses can support a country's climate goals in many ways. They can reduce their energy consumption and adopt renewable energy sources, monitor their carbon footprint, limit their waste, and use sustainable materials to create their products.

Citizens in action

By joining pressure groups (where people come together to call for changes in laws, policies, and the activities of companies), citizens can show how important climate action is to them. Volunteers in environmental organizations, such as Friends of the Earth and Greenpeace, raise awareness of environmental issues and urge leaders to take action.

Protecting the planet

People, organizations, and governments need to work together to protect the plants and animals that share the planet with us and save and restore the diverse habitats in which they live. We need to find a balance between our needs and those of the environment.

Preservation and conservation

An increasing human population has created a growing demand for Earth's natural resources, which are limited. We must find ways to achieve a balance between meeting our own needs and protecting the needs of the environment. Preservation and conservation are two ways that can help protect the environment. Preservation means setting aside areas so far untouched by humans and stopping human activity in these places to ensure that they stay unspoiled. Conservation means protecting the environment for future generations, while acknowledging the need for a certain amount of responsible human activity—for instance, by using sustainable fishing methods that allow fish populations in an area to recover rather than depleting them.

> All of us have to share the Earth's fragile ecosystems and precious resources, and each of us has a role to play in preserving them.
>
> **Kofi Annan** (former UN secretary-general), Earth Day, 2001

What can be done

Efforts by individuals and communities, government programs, and international action are all needed to repair the damage we've caused to the environment, while carefully managing Earth's natural resources for the future. Saving and restoring habitats are essential to protecting Earth's natural ecosystems and allowing wildlife to thrive. With so many species on the brink of extinction, quick and timely action is needed.

Support wildlife
Wildlife parks and marine reserves protect many plant and animal species by maintaining their habitats as safe spaces. Visiting these parks can encourage governments to continue funding them. Governments can also introduce stricter laws to save trees from being cut down and protect animals against hunting, poaching, and wildlife trafficking.

Restore habitats
The destruction of habitats to make way for buildings and farmland leaves many species struggling for survival. Restoring these habitats can slow down the damage to the environment. Citizens everywhere can help in different ways—by planting trees; putting up nesting boxes for wildlife, such as birds and insects; and making sure to never drop litter.

Working together

Conservation campaigns bring citizens together in groups to engage with a cause and create a strong voice for governments and organizations to hear. Their goals are to gather support and push governments to respond with new policies and legislation to protect the natural environment and its inhabitants. A campaign to conserve Antarctic habitats, for example, led to a marine reserve being created in 2016 in the Ross Sea, Antarctica.

Online petitions

Signing petitions is a powerful way to bring about change. Large numbers of people can show their support for action on an issue by digitally signing an online petition, which is presented to those in power to push them into action.

Connect with nature

Try to get outside! Wherever you live, you'll find a variety of plants, insects, and animals right on your doorstep. Try visiting parks or nature reserves and see what you can find. Take photographs of local plant and animal species and use a book or an app to help you identify them. To learn more about nature, read books on wildlife or watch nature documentaries on TV. Interacting with nature may inspire you to take steps to protect it.

Save water

Fresh water is essential to all plants and animals, including humans. Governments can help conserve it by introducing and enforcing laws to prevent chemical waste from getting into lakes and rivers and by restoring natural wetlands, while farmers can reduce the amount of water used in irrigation. Everyone can save water by turning off taps when not in use.

Take care of soil

Winds and rains can blow or wash away the fertile topsoil from fields. But farmers can adopt techniques to prevent soil erosion—for example, by planting new seeds and making brush dams to trap the nutrient-rich soil across gullies. Everyone can help take care of the soil by picking up litter and using food waste to make compost pits, if possible.

Switch to renewable resources

Fossil fuels, used to power vehicles and homes, are limited sources of energy and cause pollution and climate change. Governments should invest in the usage of alternative energy sources, such as solar, wind, and hydro power, which can reduce the reliance on fossil fuels. Individuals can help by walking or cycling more instead of driving cars.

Green champions

CHANGE MAKERS: ENVIRONMENTAL PROBLEMS

To preserve our planet for future generations, many young champions are working to tackle pollution, protect our land and water, and manage the effects of natural disasters. Their actions show how young people can make a difference in the fight against climate change.

Salvador Gómez-Colón

When Hurricane Maria battered Puerto Rico in 2017, it left more than a million people without electricity or clean water. This crisis spurred local teenager Salvador Gómez-Colón into action. He organized a campaign called C+Feel=Hope, where he used crowdfunding to raise nearly $200,000. He used this money to provide solar-powered lamps and hand-powered washing machines to many people in need in Puerto Rico.

Salvador Gómez-Colón was helped by his family and friends in distributing products.

Gómez-Colón distributed more than 5,000 solar-powered lamps.

About 2,000 hand-cranked washing machines were distributed.

Salman Khairalla

Most of the fresh water in Iraq comes from the Tigris and Euphrates Rivers, but over time, they have become polluted by trash, sewage, and household waste. Since 2009, Iraqi environmentalist Salman Khairalla has been committed to stopping the contamination of the rivers and the surrounding marshes and raising awareness about using water resources responsibly.

Francia Márquez

Afro-Colombian environmentalist Francia Márquez has fought against illegal gold mining in Colombia's La Toma region since 2014. Mining activities had spewed toxic chemicals in the nearby Ovejas River and caused widespread deforestation in the area. Francia organized a group of 80 women to march to the country's capital to demand government action against these activities. As a result of their protests, the Colombian government decided to stop illegal gold mining in the region.

> We're not waiting 5, 10, 20 years to take the action we want to see...we're acting now. We're not waiting any longer.
>
> **Salvador Gómez-Colón,** 50th World Economic Forum Annual Meeting, Switzerland, 2020

Amariyanna "Mari" Copeny

American teenager Mari Copeny gained widespread attention in 2016 when she wrote to then-president Barack Obama about the water crisis in her hometown of Flint, Michigan. The drinking water in the city was contaminated with lead, a toxic metal, which had come from the pipes carrying the water to people's homes. Mari's campaign to raise awareness about this water crisis pushed the government to work toward replacing the lead pipes across the city with those made of safer materials.

Gómez-Colón's initiative has helped nearly 3,500 families in Puerto Rico.

Fionn Ferreira

Plastic litter on his local coastline inspired Irish inventor Fionn Ferreira to take action. After realizing the harmful effects of tiny plastic particles called microplastics, he created a method to extract them from water in a safe and efficient manner. Fionn's invention can be used to clean the wastewater in sewage facilities before it is released into the oceans.

Be a green champion

As global citizens, we share responsibility for our environment. Everyone can make a difference by living in a greener or more environmentally friendly way. Even little changes in and around your home and in your community can matter and inspire others to act too.

Inside your home

You can be environmentally conscious right at home. Remember to follow the three Rs—reduce, reuse, and recycle. Cut down waste by reducing the amount you use at home, reusing products instead of replacing them, and recycling things. Do your part to reduce the amount of energy used in your home by turning off lights and electrical appliances when you aren't using them.

> Each and every one of us makes a difference each and every day.... What kind of difference are we going to make?
>
> **Dr. Jane Goodall** (British biologist), in a speech at Concordia University, Quebec, Canada, 2014

Solar panels installed on the roof can capture sunlight to produce electricity and power the home.

Use sunlight during the daytime as much as possible instead of turning on lights.

Don't waste water by leaving the tap running when you are washing dishes.

Avoid disposable plastic cups and straws and try reusable or recyclable alternatives, such as those made of metal or cardboard.

Reduce your electricity consumption by turning off the lights when you are not in the room.

To minimize food waste, buy only what you plan to eat and try to find new ways to use leftovers.

Save energy by turning off electronic devices and appliances if you are not using them.

Outside your home

If you have access to a yard or other outdoor space, or even just a windowsill, you can make your surroundings greener. Spend time planting flowers and trees to attract birds, small animals, and insects. You can even set up a small feeder or water bowl to leave food and water for them. One more way to be a green champion is to avoid using gas-guzzling vehicles for short journeys. Walk or ride a bike instead, if possible.

Create compost

Separate out your organic waste, such as fruit and vegetable peel, stale bread, and dry leaves. Remember to put it into a compost bin. If you have a garden, build a compost pile by using the organic waste, leaving it to break down over time. Layer it over flower beds and watch your garden grow.

Walking or riding a bike is an environmentally friendly way to travel and also helps you stay active.

Put recyclables—including glass, plastic, paper, and metal—into one or more recycling bins, based on your local guidelines.

Set up nest boxes for birds to lay their eggs in a safe place.

Grow flowers in your garden or even on your windowsill to attract insects. They help spread pollen, causing more flowers to grow.

Different kinds of waste may or may not be separated into different colored bins, based on your area. In some countries, you may have to throw food and organic waste, known as wet waste, into the same bin.

All other trash that can't be recycled goes in a separate bin.

Use homemade compost to grow vegetables in your garden if you have one, or try growing vegetables in your kitchen.

Air-dry clothes outside or on clothing racks instead of using tumble dryers.

In your community

Find out whether there are any organizations in your community working to clean up and improve the local area. Try volunteering, or if there aren't any organizations locally, you could get together with like-minded friends and neighbors to set up your own!

Farmers' market
At farmers' markets, local farmers sell their fresh food, such as fruit, vegetables, and eggs. The food has been produced locally and not shipped or flown in from another country.

Community gardening
In this type of sustainable farming, community members join their neighbors in growing food, often without using insect-killing chemicals known as pesticides.

Volunteer to help out at community gardens.

Hybrid or electric cars reduce the emission of harmful greenhouse gases, and sharing trips by carpooling reduces the number of cars on the road.

Green consumerism

Raised awareness of environmental issues has led shoppers to demand products that have less plastic, reduced packaging, and the option to reuse or recycle. This approach to shopping is called green consumerism. One of the best ways to help the environment, however, is to buy less and only what you need.

> The truth is our planet's alarm is now going off, and it's time to finally wake up and take action.
>
> **Leonardo DiCaprio** (American actor), as Earth Day Chairman, 2000

Buying green
When buying a green product, be cautious about whether it is actually eco-friendly. To attract environmentally conscious shoppers, many products are advertised as being eco-friendly by using words such as "organic" and "cruelty-free," but this may not always be true. Do some research online in advance of going to the stores to help you make informed choices.

Kids Against Plastic

Sisters Amy and Ella Meek started the Kids Against Plastic campaign in the UK to raise awareness of the problems caused by single-use plastic. The teenagers help people find alternatives to plastic, while encouraging schools and businesses to reduce their use of plastics.

Public transit

If your trip is too far to walk, see whether you can use public transit. Buses and trains are a more environmentally friendly option, and in some places, buses are powered by electricity. If more people used public transportation, fewer cars would be on the road.

Picking up litter

Unfortunately, some places have problems with litter. Try to join litter-collecting groups, which remove trash to keep their local areas clean.

Help the environment

Diminishing natural resources, pollution, and endangered species are just some of the big problems we must solve. Governments and global organizations, such as Greenpeace and the World Wildlife Fund (WWF), are trying to find solutions, but every global citizen can take action on the issues affecting our environment.

Donations
Donate unwanted clothes, toys, and appliances to a thrift store where they will help those in need, instead of throwing them away.

Fundraisers
Plan a community fundraiser, such as a fun run or a bake sale, and use the earnings to support an environmental charity.

Petitions and protests
Consider important issues that affect where you live. Sign or start petitions to support existing local green spaces or create new ones, for example.

Blogs and websites
Write a blog describing how you are going green. Contact local newspapers or websites to spread the word to the wider community.

Our digital lives

NAVIGATING THE INTERNET AND ONLINE COMMUNITIES

66 Ours is a networked, globalized society connected by new technologies. The Internet is the tool we use to interact with one another and accordingly poses new challenges to privacy and security. **99**

Zaryn Dentzel (founder and CEO of Tuenti), "How the Internet Has Changed Everyday Life" in *Ch@nge: 19 Key Essays on How Internet is Changing our Lives*, 2013

Media

Media refers to the various ways of communicating information to people, through newspapers, television, radio, and the Internet. In the past, it often took days or even months for news to travel, but now information can be reported around the world almost instantly.

Types of media

The media covers all forms of news as well as content related to entertainment, business, and education. Older or traditional forms of media include print publishing as well as radio and television. More recent forms include websites and apps.

Print
Newspapers, journals, magazines, billboards, and flyers

Radio
Radio channels

Television and cinema
Television channels and movies

Digital
Websites, digital apps, podcasts, and social media

Different kinds of media can report on the same event.

Role of media

No matter its form, the media has many functions—from sharing the facts about current events with the public to providing platforms to citizens for voicing their concerns.

> A free press...a pillar of democracy.
> **Nelson Mandela** (former South African president), 1999

Holding people accountable
The media often questions politicians and powerful people about how their decisions and actions affect society.

Informing people
The media tells people about what is happening in the world around them.

Highlighting important issues
The media brings key issues to the public's attention in order to raise awareness.

Connecting people
The speed of social media enables people all over the world to contact each other and share information in an instant.

Freedom of the media

When the people and platforms that report information are free to do their job without interference, they can reveal the true story of events and share it transparently with people, highlight issues of concern, and challenge elected leaders. Some governments control what information reaches the public by censoring the media.

Using media responsibly

People have a responsibility to question the accuracy, truth, and origins of the information they consume and ensure that it is accurate before sharing it. Some content can be deliberately misleading or biased. Think carefully about what you read, watch, and listen to, and check information from different sources.

Misinformation
False information is easy to come across on the Internet because content is often not monitored by any one neutral body.

Biases
News articles are often affected by a writer's biases, presenting information in a certain way to persuade people of something.

Lack of diversity
A lack of diversity in news media may mean that stories about a particular group are prioritized at the expense of other groups. Inclusive reporting means that all groups in society should be fairly represented.

Who influences media?

The media is not always able to report information or opinions freely—instead, it may be used by those in power, such as politicians or businesses, as a tool to control the flow of information to citizens. This may mean that information reported by the media is not always complete or trustworthy.

Corporate and political influence
Politicians and corporations may influence or try to hide part of a story or report from the public to protect themselves or for their own gain.

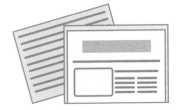

Advertising influence
Many media organizations receive money from advertisers for displaying their ads online or in newspapers where readers can see them. Advertisers in turn may make demands about the types of content that can be included.

GET INVOLVED
Become a citizen journalist

Journalists work to gather information about events or issues—they then share it with the public. With the Internet giving people access to news at any time of the day or night and the ability to publish your own content online, people can now act as citizen journalists by playing their own part in reporting and analysing current events independently. You can get involved by reporting on something that happened in your school or interviewing someone for a blog or your school website. Be sure to report the facts accurately!

Fake news

False or misleading information, often called fake news, presented as fact is everywhere today. When consuming information online, it's essential to question the sources of the news, to seek out different points of view, and to try to have a balanced understanding of what's happening.

SEE ALSO	
❮ **126–127** Media	
Communicating online	**130–131 ❯**
Being an online citizen	**134–135 ❯**

What is misinformation?

Misinformation, commonly known as fake news, can be deliberately misleading to discredit or cause harm to an individual, organization, or group. If misinformation is shared, it can take on a life of its own—something that's false can appear true if lots of people are sharing it.

Spotting fake news
It can be challenging, but while reading news, there are simple questions you can ask yourself in order to separate fact from fiction.

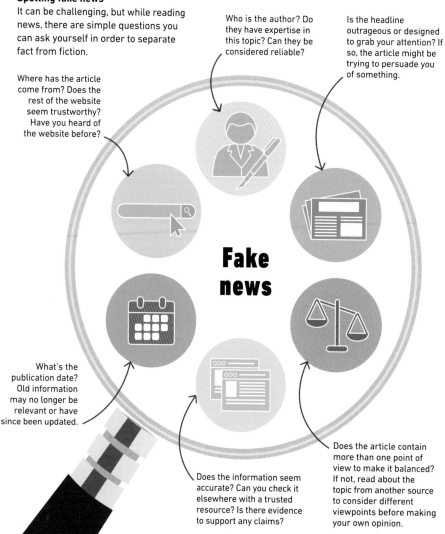

Who is the author? Do they have expertise in this topic? Can they be considered reliable?

Is the headline outrageous or designed to grab your attention? If so, the article might be trying to persuade you of something.

Where has the article come from? Does the rest of the website seem trustworthy? Have you heard of the website before?

Fake news

What's the publication date? Old information may no longer be relevant or have since been updated.

Does the information seem accurate? Can you check it elsewhere with a trusted resource? Is there evidence to support any claims?

Does the article contain more than one point of view to make it balanced? If not, read about the topic from another source to consider different viewpoints before making your own opinion.

Types of misinformation

A news story not matching your beliefs may not be fake news. But there are many types of fake news—from articles that leave out information to stories that may be exaggerated or sensationalized. It's important to double-check information before believing or sharing it.

Satire or parody
This content is not designed to cause harm but has potential to fool readers into thinking it is true.

Misleading content
When facts are left out, intentionally or unintentionally, the content becomes misleading.

Imposter content
Fake sources may pretend to be an official and authoritative source while sharing content that is false.

Manipulated content
This content aims to deliberately deceive readers by changing or leaving out genuine information.

Fabricated content
The content is entirely false and is written to deceive readers and cause harm.

What's behind fake news?

Fake news can be used to influence people's views and encourage a particular reaction from them. Some global media organizations are controlled by powerful individuals and companies. They may have a political agenda or seek to control the flow of information to the public, resulting in biased or misleading information being circulated. Additionally, some people create fake news in order to encourage people to click on their websites so that they can make money from clicks.

Propaganda
Politicians and other powerful individuals can influence public opinion by using the media to spread propaganda, which is biased information to promote a person's cause or point of view.

Foreign influences
One country or government may manipulate social media by spreading fake news to have an impact on the politics in another country.

Business interests
Some media organizations may publish misleading information because they want to make a profit. They earn money from advertising and might not want to report negative news about a company that is paying to advertise with them.

Social media bubbles

Social media platforms are designed to track a person's browsing habits to figure out the types of content most likely to interest them. While this can be good, as you don't have to see content you aren't interested in, it also means that you only get to hear one side of a story. Not hearing about other people's perspectives is called a "social media bubble." This "bubble" effect means it's easy to miss important information and other points of view and for incorrect information to circulate widely. To escape your social media bubble, look for information in different places, including content that disagrees with your beliefs.

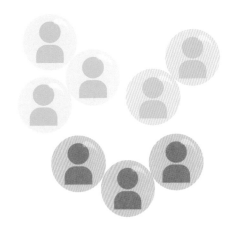

Informed opinions

With the amount of information available today, it is more important than ever for people to try to separate facts from fake news and form opinions only after checking information across a range of sources.

Consider how an article is written and whether it contains verifiable facts or is making general, vague statements.

Think about the intention behind the article and the reason why the author has written it. What is the author's agenda?

Look for detailed coverage that provides enough evidence to ensure that you are getting the full story. Look for a balanced outline of viewpoints.

Communicating online

The digital age has transformed communication in incredible ways. People can now talk to each other instantly via many different online platforms on computers, laptops, tablets, and smartphones.

Your digital self

People can choose to present themselves in different ways online, depending on which digital platform they are using. An online profile on a social media platform with friends may look very different from a professional profile on a work or business site. An individual may have multiple online identities, each linked to how they use the Internet.

The Internet

The Internet is a vast source of information, education, and entertainment as well as a place to socialize with friends without even leaving the house.

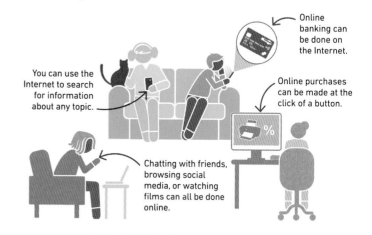

Online banking can be done on the Internet.

You can use the Internet to search for information about any topic.

Online purchases can be made at the click of a button.

Chatting with friends, browsing social media, or watching films can all be done online.

Many ways to communicate

The Internet, with its wide range of platforms, lets people do many different things—from staying in touch to learning more about the world and working with one another to achieve shared goals.

Build social communities
People with similar ideas and interests can meet online to learn from each other or form communities that pursue shared goals.

Connect with people
People use social media to connect with family and friends. Message boards or discussion forums are also popular for sharing ideas, images, videos, and comments.

Share information
There is a huge amount of information available to read and share, including online books and encyclopedias, articles, journals, and blogs.

Social media

Online communities can form when people communicate on social media, including such platforms as Twitter, Facebook, Instagram, LinkedIn, YouTube, Snapchat, TikTok, Pinterest, Tumblr, and Reddit. Social media is also great for sharing content, discovering information, and arranging events.

#Hashtag

Today, many campaigns on social media platforms start with a hashtag—a pound sign (#) followed by a keyword. This collects online content relevant to the topic or keyword, making it easier for people to find. Hashtags that trend (become popular) can reach a huge, even global, audience. Following or using a hashtag may be the first step in joining an online campaign. Hashtags may also be used on signs in in-person protests to draw attention to a cause—**#Enough** sums up the feelings of frustration about gun violence in schools in the US.

Create awareness
Raising awareness of important issues on a local or global scale is made possible by social media apps, discussion forums, and online petitions.

We are all now connected by the Internet, like neurons in a giant brain.
Stephen Hawking (English scientist), *USA Today*, 2014

Network professionally
Working professionals use networking sites to connect with people from similar backgrounds and find out about employment opportunities.

Generate support
People can gather interest and support as well as donations for different causes by using online crowdsourcing tools and social media apps.

Online champions

CHANGE MAKERS: ONLINE SAFETY

With more than half of the global population now using the Internet, the problems of fake news, cyberbullying, and trolling are widespread. Thankfully, there are some young netizens (Internet citizens) leading the way with apps and campaigns to limit negative content on the Internet and support victims of online hate.

Trisha Prabhu

A victim of cyberbullying herself, American teenager Trisha Prabhu was inspired to take action in 2013 when she read about a young girl who had taken her own life because of online bullying. She developed ReThink™—an app that tries to stop cyberbullying before it happens. The app detects offensive messages before they've been sent and gives the sender a chance to reconsider their actions. The app has made many users change their minds before posting hateful messages online.

Sadat Rahman raises the Children's Peace Prize trophy.

Sadat Rahman

Bangladeshi student Sadat Rahman designed a mobile app called Cyber Teens to help young people who are facing bullying online. The app enables victims of cyberbullying in Narail, Bangladesh, to contact a team of volunteers who report the crimes to local police and social workers. Sadat won the International Children's Peace Prize in 2020 for his groundbreaking app.

> Serious action needs to be taken right now. Teenagers continue to remain vulnerable to online crime and cyberbullying.
>
> **Sadat Rahman**, Interview with *AFP*, 2020

BE INFORMED

No Hate Speech Movement

The youth campaign "No hate speech movement" was started by the Council of Europe Youth Department in 2013, and it ran for four years across 45 countries. The campaign made young people aware of online hate speech and encouraged them to fight back against abusive, threatening, or discriminatory content. By working with governments, the movement made efforts to combat intolerance online and offline and set up platforms for reporting hate speech.

Gitanjali Rao

Selected as *TIME* magazine's "Kid of the Year" for 2020, American scientist and inventor Gitanjali Rao wants to build a community of young innovators to help solve problems around the world by using technology. She created an anti-cyberbullying service called Kindly, which detects words or phrases most commonly used by online bullies. Gitanjali is a member of the Children's Kindness Network, an organization that teaches young children about the value of kindness to combat bullying both online and offline.

Ash Ball

Anti-cyberbullying campaigner Ash Ball is part of Australia's Project Rockit movement, which provides interactive school workshops to help young people stand up to online hate and prejudice. To expand the reach of this program, Ash launched a YouTube channel with videos for students, parents, and teachers around the world. The videos cover such issues as privacy, hate in online gaming, and the pressure to be perfect in today's digital world.

Paula Côrte Real

Brazilian lawyer Paula Côrte Real wants to ensure that the Internet is a safe and secure place for young people to express themselves without worrying about hate or bullying. She has helped with several youth engagement programs that teach students how to protect themselves while using the Internet and how to safely tackle cyberstalking and cyberbullying. Paula was awarded the Internet Society's 25 under 25 award in 2017, which acknowledged the impact of her work on her community and beyond.

Being an online citizen

Each of us has a responsibility to be respectful toward others and to protect our privacy when using the Internet. Even though posting something online may take just a second, it's important to think carefully before doing so.

Online etiquette

Good online etiquette means you should be as polite, kind, and truthful online as you are in your community. If all online users behaved respectfully when sending messages, posting on social media, or commenting on discussions, it would help make the digital world a safe and positive place. Unfortunately, not all Internet users are honest or behave appropriately, so be careful online not to post personal information and to avoid disturbing or offensive content.

Be respectful toward others
You can hurt someone's feelings if you write mean things about them online. Be respectful toward other people in just the same way you would if you were together in person.

Do not copy without permission
Do not use pictures or text without requesting permission first. It is against the law to take other people's work and claim it as your own.

Be wary of spam
Spam includes unwanted and potentially harmful ads, messages, or emails. Setting controls can reduce the amount of spam you receive. Be sure never to send it to someone else.

Do not download illegally
Piracy (downloading or distributing digital content without permission) is illegal in most countries. Doing so means you are stealing and not paying the creator for their work.

How to stay safe online

The Internet is an amazing tool for getting help with school work, socializing with friends, and being entertained, but it's important to be careful when using it. It is essential when you're online to take steps to protect your identity and personal information.

Protect your devices
Install the latest software packages to safeguard your laptops and mobile phones from viruses and malware. Also, update your webcam security so hackers cannot access your devices. Always ask an adult to help with setting up your online security.

Use appropriate privacy settings
Update your privacy settings on social media to hide your personal information. From email accounts to banking information used for online shopping, personal data can be stolen by hackers who use it for identity theft, bank raids, or cyber attacks.

Avoid dangerous content
The Internet contains inappropriate and potentially harmful content, such as violence and pornography. Steer clear of unfamiliar sites to stay safe. Beware of strangers online, as you don't know their true identities.

Protect your data
Do not click on suspicious links or pop-ups you don't recognize, as they can be set up to infect your computer with viruses or used to steal sensitive data, including personal photos and passwords.

Extreme views

Some people use the Internet to spread their prejudiced and potentially harmful opinions to as many people as they can. The anonymity of online communication makes this easy. Rather than accepting someone else's opinion, do your own research. Get your information from trustworthy sources and be wary of people sharing extreme views.

Listening to all sides
In online debates and chats, give all sides careful thought and consideration before forming your own opinions.

Cyberbullying

Bullies in the online world can send hurtful or intimidating messages and comments, share embarrassing photos or personal information, or even take over a person's online identity by creating a fake social media profile. If someone is experiencing cyberbullying, there are steps they can take to get help and tackle this problem.

If you are a victim of cyberbullying, block and report the bully to the website where they are operating.

Save screenshots of aggressive or unpleasant messages as evidence of cyberbullying.

Tell family members, friends, or teachers to make them aware of what is happening and share how you feel.

Contact a helpline for young people dealing with issues like cyberbullying to get advice and support.

Calling all global citizens

MAKING OUR WORLD BETTER FOR ALL

" Do it! What are you waiting on? Do it! Stand up for what you believe in. The world needs your voice. Whoever you are, you have something to say. Say it. **"**

Kerry Washington (American actor), Interview with *Women's Health* magazine, 2014

Find your cause

As you learn more about what's happening in your community and the world, you might discover a problem or cause you feel strongly about. Finding a cause that matters to you may make you want to take action.

What do you care about?

Every day, many young global citizens are making a difference by campaigning or volunteering for a cause that matters to them. Some of these issues are local, while others affect the whole world. In this book, you've learned about different issues, and this might have inspired you to want to act. While it might seem difficult to pick one cause among so many, think about what interests you most and perhaps ask friends or relatives what causes they care about too. As you begin to explore these local and global issues to find the one that matters most to you, here are some suggestions to get you started.

Animal welfare
Stray animals on the streets or those in rescue centers need attention. Volunteer at your local animal shelter to help feed or nurture these animals or raise funds to support them.

Clean-up drives
Litter and trash pollute the land. You could participate in clean-up days in your community during which citizens get together to clean up their local area.

Helping the homeless
Some people can end up losing their homes because of difficult circumstances. Volunteering at food banks and in homeless shelters is one way of helping people in need.

Education for all
Consider volunteering at local schools or libraries to become a homework helper, tutor, or classroom assistant. This means you can help more people discover a love of learning.

Wildlife conservation
Many animals are endangered in the wild
and are protected in nature parks. Visit
these parks if you can and help raise
money for a charity that supports
wildlife conservation.

Assisting the elderly
Many elderly people in your community
may be living on their own or in nursing homes.
Volunteer to help elderly people with
their everyday chores or just spend
time talking with them.

Climate action
Climate change affects all of us. Reducing
household waste and encouraging
your family to walk more instead
of taking the car are small ways
to combat climate change.

Planting trees
With wildlife habitats being destroyed,
every tree planted helps counter
the problem. Start a campaign with
your friends to plant new trees.

Combating discrimination
Take action to support people who may
experience discrimination based on their
identity. Read about different issues affecting
marginalized communities and help
people in your community or school
become more aware.

Human rights
Many groups of people still have to fight
for their basic human rights. Research
the subject of human rights and volunteer
with an organization that
spreads awareness.

Digital safety
Young people may struggle to manage
the information they share on the Internet.
Campaign with your friends using posters
with tips on making safe choices
online to empower teens.

Plan and prepare

SEE ALSO

❮ **16–17** Who is a citizen?

❮ **18–19** Are we global citizens?

❮ **138–139** Find your cause

Make a difference   **142–143** ❯

Now that you have found a cause to focus on, it's time to make a plan of action. Whether your goal is to organize a bake sale or a campaign, do your research, get support from others, and remember you're not alone!

Get going

Start by exploring your chosen cause and finding out as much as you can. If you would like to get involved, think about how and what your goals might be. Would you like to organize a fundraising event or raise awareness of your cause among friends, family, or your community? If you have time, you might like to become a volunteer with a local charity or organization related to your cause or even decide to start your own organization!

1 **Gather information**
Doing research online can help you find out what other people and organizations are doing for the cause you care about at local and global levels.

2 **Reach out**
A trusted adult, such as a parent or a teacher, can help you make contact with others who support the same cause. Social media can help you find like-minded people.

Thinking about the future

If you are really passionate about a cause, you could build your whole future career around it. By picking subjects in school that relate to the issues you care about, your studies can help you find a job in that area when you're older. Although it's not the only way to make a difference, working in areas related to your cause can give you the knowledge and power to make a big impact.

A social worker or counselor might have studied sociology or psychology to improve their understanding of people.

Someone studying biology or environmental science could become a conservationist who works to preserve and protect wildlife.

I had to ask strangers to join me and one another on real-life projects—fixing up a park...or starting an after-school program.

Barack Obama (former US president), *A Promised Land*, 2020

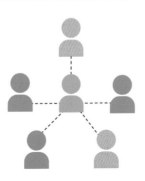

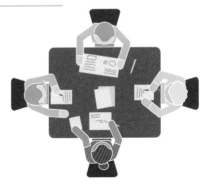

3 Make a plan
You can make a plan on your own or together with someone else. Think about what your goals are and when you want to achieve them by.

4 Find support
Achieving your goals is much easier if you have some help! Try to find charities that can offer you support. A teacher or a parent could help you get in touch with them.

5 Keep trying!
Remember, you're not alone—you're part of a larger community of committed global citizens who all want to make a difference. Learn from others and keep trying together.

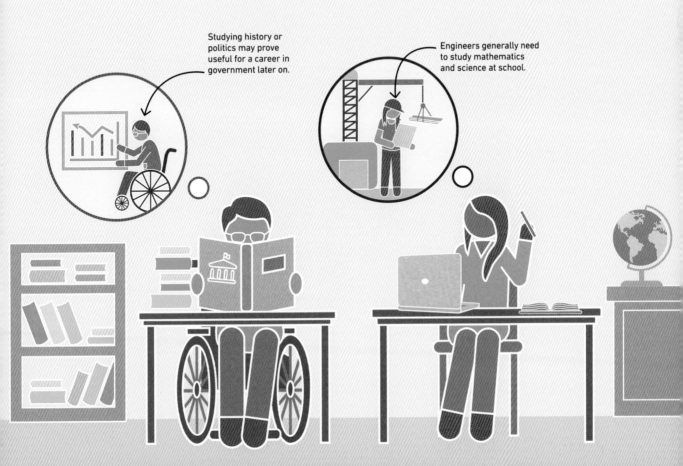

Studying history or politics may prove useful for a career in government later on.

Engineers generally need to study mathematics and science at school.

Make a difference

Think how much better the world could be if every single person did their part. Each person has the power to make a difference. As a global citizen, you can make an impact, even with small actions.

Take action

Once you've got your cause in mind and your plan in place, it's time to take action. Whether you choose to start something new or join an existing campaign or movement, there is a lot you can do. From organizing local fundraisers for people needing support to leading a campaign for creating a new local green space, your actions will combine with those taken by other young global citizens, making an impact on a large scale.

SEE ALSO

⟨ 18–19 Are we global citizens?
⟨ 52–53 Power to the people
⟨ 120–123 Be a green champion
⟨ 130–131 Communicating online
⟨ 140–141 Plan and prepare

> Don't be intimidated by what you think you can't do. Do what you can.
>
> **Kallan Benson** (American climate advocate), interview with *Sierra*, 2019

Social media
Share an important post or meaningful hashtag on social media to lend your support to your chosen cause. Make sure the post has come from a source you can trust.

Letters and emails
You can write letters or emails to local media or to a local politician to draw their attention to your chosen cause.

Direct appeals
Many businesses may be associated with charities. They may listen to feedback from the public. With the help of a trusted adult, contact a local business to ask them to support your cause.

Raise awareness
By making and distributing leaflets and posters in your local community, you can share information about your cause with others.

Boycott
You could stop using the products or services of a company that you don't agree with. Talk to people around you to explain why, and perhaps they may also do the same.

Speak to people
By attending an event, such as a meeting or a protest, related to your cause, you can talk to like-minded people who are also hoping to bring about change.

Global citizens together

Local efforts at the community level can sometimes become global movements as awareness grows on the news and social media. In 2018, Swedish schoolgirl Greta Thunberg's solo protest against climate change was the first step toward the formation of a new global movement, which now has supporters in almost 150 countries.

Crowdfunding
Using purpose-built websites and apps, people can raise lots of small donations from others around the world for a charity or specific cause.

Hashtag campaigns
Online campaigns can be started when people share hashtags related to a cause on social media to show their support. As more people follow the hashtag and share it, the chain of support will continue to grow.

Crowdsourcing
New projects or campaigns can be launched by sourcing ideas, information, and services from a large group of interested people on social media and the Internet.

Worldwide networks
Some international organizations encourage young people to volunteer for local causes, such as planting trees or fundraising for communities in need. When volunteers in different locations help out, they can have a global impact.

Every action counts

People may sometimes think that making a difference involves bringing about change on a global scale, but even small differences can lift community spirit and change lives. Working together, we can all make the world more fair and sustainable for everyone.

Local clean-up
You could organize a clean-up with your family and friends where you live. When there are lots of people to help, the task can be done quickly, and you will soon see improvements in your local area.

BE INFORMED

Young heroes

There are many young heroes already making a difference in their local communities. One example is American schoolgirl Hailey Richman (below right), who organizes fun events where local kids spend time solving jigsaw puzzles with patients suffering memory loss caused by Alzheimer's disease.

7

The US

Politics and government

The United States is a federal republic in North America, made up
of fifty states, Washington, D.C., five self-governing territories, and
a few islands.

The United States of America

The large map shows the mainland US, which
is made of 48 states and Washington, D.C. The
D.C. stands for District of Columbia—this is a
federal district that houses the capital of the US.
Seen at the bottom are the states of Alaska—
separated from the mainland by Canada—
and Hawaii, which is a chain of islands in the
Pacific Ocean. Not shown on these maps are the
country's self-governing territories—American
Samoa, Guam, and the Northern Mariana
Islands in the Pacific; and Puerto Rico and
the US Virgin Islands in the Atlantic Ocean.

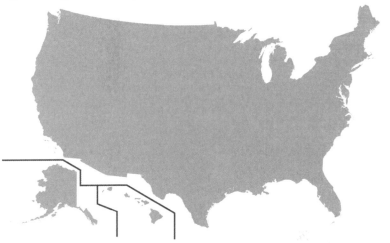

A Federal Presidential Constitutional Republic

In this example of representative democracy, a constitution guides the government, which has three
branches with checks and balances on each other's power—the legislative, judiciary, and executive branches.
In the US, the national government shares power with the state governments, which is called a federation.

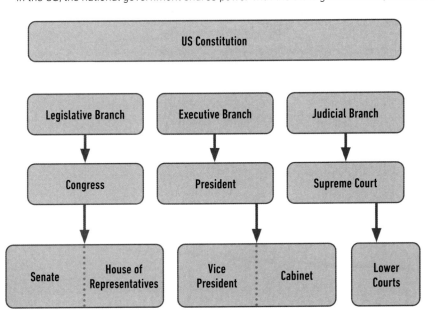

The United States Constitution

Ratified in 1788, the written
constitution of the US is the
oldest in the world that's still
in use. It replaced the older
Articles of Confederation, which
didn't unify the interests of
the various states. It consists
of seven articles, which lay out
the structure of the federal
government. The US Constitution
also famously includes a Bill
of Rights, which spells out the
fundamental rights of US citizens.

Political parties

The United States has several political parties, each with its own views and goals. However, elected federal officials (officials of the national or federal government) are almost exclusively from only two major parties—the Democratic and the Republican parties. Third-party candidates usually play a limited "spoiler" role, drawing votes away from the major party candidates.

The Democratic Party
Founded in 1828, this is one of the two major parties in the US. A liberal party, it has a progressive social liberal platform and promotes civil liberty and social equality.

The Libertarian Party
This party was founded in 1971 and favors limited government.

The Green Party
Formed in 2001, this party promotes environmentalism and is against racism and war.

The Republican Party
Founded in 1854, the Grand Old Party (GOP), as it is also known, is the other of the two major parties in the country. It advocates for an American form of conservatism.

The Constitution Party
Dating from 1990, this party promotes a religious and conservative view of the Constitution.

Congressional districts
Each of the fifty states in the country is divided into congressional districts. Each state has two senators who serve in the Senate (for a total of 100 people). Each congressional district within each state elects someone to serve in the House of Representatives. There are 435 representatives.

Congressional districts can change rapidly in the U.S. For example, Virginia's 7th District has typically been a Republican district but was won by the Democrats in 2018. It remained with the Democrats in 2020.

Elections

In the US, elections are held for many different levels of government. Congressional elections (elections for Senate and House seats) are won by the candidates who win the most votes. In a presidential election, after the popular vote, members of a body called the Electoral College (known as electors) vote for the president. Each state and the District of Columbia has a specific number of electors. In most states, the party that wins the popular vote gets their electors to cast all the state's electoral votes for its presidential candidate. Most elected terms begin in January of the year after the election.

1 Registering to vote
In the US, only citizens who are 18 years of age or older may vote. Every state has different rules for registering to vote. Each person must register themselves to vote.

2 Placing a vote
Votes can be cast by citizens on paper or electronic ballots at their local, assigned precincts or sent in by mail (as an absentee ballot) for special preapproved reasons, such as chronic illness.

Who heads the government?

The candidate who wins the Electoral College vote becomes the president of the United States and forms the executive branch of the federal government. The president appoints qualified people to run the departments of government as secretaries, who set the federal policies and priorities. The Senate approves many of these appointments. The departments are run by civil servants, who are often career employees who do not leave when an administration ends and a new one begins.

The President of the United States (POTUS)
The head of the state and the government, the president of the United States leads the executive branch of the federal government and also serves as the commander-in-chief of the Armed Forces.

The Vice President
The vice president is second in line for the presidency and steps in to lead the country if the president is incapacitated. The vice president is also the president of the Senate and can cast a tie-breaking vote there.

The Attorney General
Called the nation's highest-ranking legal adviser, the attorney general leads the Department of Justice, pursues law enforcement cases on behalf of the nation, and advises the president on matters of law.

Secretaries of State and Defense
The Secretary of State, who leads the US Department of State, is the chief diplomat of the nation and implements the government's foreign policy. As the head of the Department of Defense, the Secretary of Defense has command of the US Armed Forces and is second only to the president.

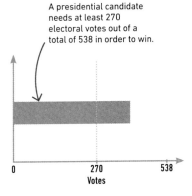

A presidential candidate needs at least 270 electoral votes out of a total of 538 in order to win.

0   270   538
Votes

3 **The popular vote**
Votes are counted by hand or machine. In a presidential election, after the counting of votes, every state and the District of Columbia have a majority for a candidate.

4 **The Electoral College**
In the presidential election, each state and the District of Columbia receive a set number of votes in the Electoral College, which elects the president. A candidate can win the popular vote but lose the Electoral College vote.

5 **Forming the Cabinet**
The president-elect chooses a Cabinet based on their priorities for each department of the government. The Cabinet includes the Secretaries of State, Defense, and Education, with 24 members in all.

The United States Congress

Consisting of two equal houses of elected officials, the U.S. Congress is the legislative branch of the American government.

The two houses

The US Congress is divided into two parts or houses: the House of Representatives and the Senate. The Senate serves as the upper chamber, and the House of Representatives is the lower chamber. They both meet in the US Capitol in Washington, D.C.

The Speaker of the House is elected by the majority party of the House and presides over it.

The two main parties (the Democrats and the Republicans) sit together in the same sections of the room.

Well of the House

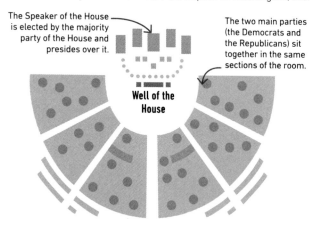

House of Representatives
The 435 members of the House are elected to two-year terms. They can propose and approve bills, debate laws and policies, declare war, and debate the president's budget. Both chambers of Congress must vote to approve bills before they become law.

The vice president of the United States presides over the Senate and casts tie-breaking votes when needed.

Democrats   Republicans

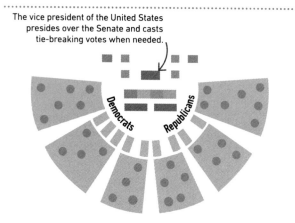

The Senate
The 100 senators are elected to six-year terms. The Senate's responsibilities are similar to the House's, although the Senate has special duties, including approving the president's cabinet and conducting trials of presidents impeached by the House. As the smaller house, the Senate is considered the more prestigious legislative body.

Making laws

The process during which a proposed bill becomes an actual law in the United States is a complex one, often involving both the executive and legislative branches.

Bill is introduced
A bill is introduced in either the House or the Senate. The presiding officer then assigns the bill to an appropriate committee.

Committee stage
The committee meets to discuss, amend, and vote on the bill. It can be approved or tabled (postponed) for later.

Voting by the house
If a bill passes committee, it comes to the full house floor, where it is debated and amended before it is brought to a vote.

Passed to the other house
A bill passed by either the House or the Senate is then sent to the other house for debate and approval.

Committee stage
In the other house, the process begins again. The bill is sent to a committee where it's discussed, amended, and either approved or tabled.

Final debate
Once approved by the committee, it is brought to the floor for a final debate, amendments, and a vote.

Considering amendments
If amendments are made, they're sent back to the first house for approval. Once the changes are made, a final bill is then approved.

Presidential approval
Once both houses approve a bill, it's sent to the president, who has ten days to either sign the bill or veto it.

Overriding a veto
If a bill is vetoed (sent back to the Congress) by the president, Congress can override the veto with a two-thirds majority vote. Once approved, the bill becomes a law.

Citizens of the US

As a citizen of the United States, you are entitled to certain rights and benefits and are expected to perform certain duties as well.

Being a US citizen

A US citizen is a legally recognized member of the country. Any person born within US territory is entitled to American citizenship, as are some who have legally lived and worked in the country for at least five years. Citizens are protected by the Constitution and guaranteed many freedoms in its Bill of Rights, such as freedom of speech and religion. American citizens also have the right to vote.

Healthcare
The US has no national healthcare system for everyone. A system called Medicaid helps people with low or no income, while Medicare helps the elderly.

Education
Children of citizens and noncitizens alike have access to free primary and secondary public education, and school is required until the age of 18.

Welfare system
The welfare system provides food assistance, supplementary income, and unemployment benefits for all as well as Social Security for the retired.

Citizen responsibilities

American citizens have basic responsibilities, such as following the posted speed limits when driving and obeying all other laws, as well as more complex responsibilities, such as respecting others' ability to practice constitutionally granted rights, even when they disagree with them.

Serving on a jury
If called upon to serve on a jury, it's required unless doing so would cause an undue financial burden. After they have served, citizens cannot be called again for jury duty for a period of time, which varies from state to state.

Providing public information
The Freedom of Information Act (FOIA) requires full or partial disclosure of previously unreleased information and documents controlled by the US government, upon any person's request.

Registering to vote
All American citizens are encouraged to vote. Only when all citizens vote is the country a true democracy.

Paying taxes
Americans are required to not only pay income taxes but also contribute to Social Security and Medicare. These are deducted from paychecks. The income-tax rate varies based on income.

BE INFORMED

Environment plan

Joe Biden, who became president in 2021, has made combating climate change a major goal for his administration. Based in part on the Green New Deal (a plan for executing new American environmental policies to stop climate change), the Biden plan focuses on the idea that economic growth and environmental policy are connected. It aims to reduce carbon emissions, prioritize alternative forms of energy, and create jobs in the environmental sector. This is a total change from President Donald Trump's policies, which included prioritizing carbon-based fuels.

Agents of change

American society has changed greatly since the country's founding in the 1700s. Today's America better reflects the vast diversity of its people, although more change is still needed.

Pivotal Moments in American Society

Many of the most noteworthy moments that changed American society reflect the desire to be more inclusive of all people and not just those who have historically held power. America has tried to move toward better representation of all people.

1863

Emancipation Proclamation
The Emancipation Proclamation freed enslaved people in Southern states still in rebellion against the US government during the Civil War.

1865

13th and 14th Amendments
While the 13th Amendment officially ended slavery in the US by codifying its end in the Constitution, the 14th Amendment gave full citizenship to Black men.

1916

National Park Service
The National Park Service was created to manage the growing number of National Parks in the US, a program begun by President Teddy Roosevelt in 1906.

1964

The Civil Rights Act 1964
This act outlawed discrimination based on race, color, religion, sex, national origin, and later sexual orientation and gender identity. It was followed in 1965 by the Voting Rights Act, which prevented racial discrimination in voting.

1935

The Social Security Act 1935
Signed into law by President Franklin D. Roosevelt, this act provided federal welfare programs for the poor and income for the elderly after they retire.

1920

Women's suffrage
With the passage of the 19th Amendment, women's suffrage was granted in the US to white women, meaning they could now vote.

1970

The Clean Air Act 1970
The act was signed into law by President Richard Nixon, who then created the Environmental Protection Agency to enforce it.

1973

Roe vs. Wade
The Supreme Court's decision in *Roe vs. Wade* stated that the Constitution protects a woman's right to choose to have an abortion without excessive government restriction.

2015

Same-sex marriages legalized
The Supreme Court struck down all state laws that banned same-sex marriage, legalizing it in all fifty states.

Change makers

Desmond Napoles
Desmond is an LGBTQ+ champion who emphasizes the importance of diversity, acceptance, and self-expression in people.

Emma Gonzalez
Emma co-founded a gun control campaign group after surviving a mass shooting at her school in 2018.

Isra Hirsi
This environmental champion founded the US Youth Climate Strike group to fight climate change.

Yara Shahidi
Actor Yara Shahidi takes on issues of women's empowerment by trying to address the lack of diversity in Hollywood.

Active organizations

Black Youth Project 100
This is a Black youth organization that engages in community outreach to support young Black people.

Transkids Purple Rainbow Foundation
This organization aims to empower and uplift transgender and gender-nonconforming youth.

United Students Against Sweatshops (U.S.A.S.)
Founded in 1998 to support working people, U.S.A.S. aims to end the use of child workers.

United We Dream
This organization works to improve the lives of young immigrants by providing resources, support, and education.

Find out more

These are some organizations you can look into if you need support. Many more can be found online.

Discrimination/harassment

StopHate
Dedicated to fighting prejudice, StopHate runs campaigns and provides educational resources.

The American Civil Liberties Union (ACLU)
Its mission is to ensure that the rights and liberties given in the US Constitution are realized for all.

The National Association for the Advancement of Colored People (NAACP)
Originally formed to combat racial discrimination, the NAACP works to ensure a society in which all individuals have equal rights.

The Southern Poverty Law Center (SPLC)
The SPLC monitors hate groups in the US and provides legal resources to fight them.

Gender and sexual identity

InterAct
This organization provides support and legal assistance to intersex children and their families.

It Gets Better
This online resource aims to empower LGBTQ+ youth in the US and around the globe.

National Domestic Violence Hotline
This organization provides support, help, and local resources to people experiencing domestic violence.

The Trevor Project
Creators of a handbook on coming out, they provide other valuable services, such as a support helpline.

Online help

Internet Safety 101
This organization offers information on how predators use the Internet to lure kids, among other cybersafety topics.

KidsHealth.Org
This site has resources for teens about staying safe online.

PACER
PACER's National Bullying Prevention Center provides resources to deal with cyberbullying.

Refugees

Refugee Council U.S.A.
This group protects, welcomes, and assists refugees in resettling when they arrive in the US.

The American Red Cross
This group aids immigrants in the US in a variety of ways, particularly during natural disasters.

US Committee for Refugees and Immigrants
It provides services to refugees and immigrants new to the US to help them settle in.

Environment

Humane Society Wildlife Land Trust (HSWLT)
The HSWLT works to protect wildlife with permanent habitats across the US.

The Sierra Club
This environmental organization has branches in all 50 states of the US. It is working to protect animals, habitats, and water resources.

Family support and health

OK2Talk
This community is for young adults struggling with mental health and includes a 24/7 hotline.

The National Parent Hotline
Open to caregivers of all ages, this organization provides emotional support and helpful information.

United Cerebral Palsy
This group provides resources for disabled people with cerebral palsy or other conditions.

Glossary

able-bodied
A person who is not disabled. Some able-bodied people may consider themselves "typical" or "normal" compared to disabled people. *see also* disabled

ableism
Discrimination faced by disabled people. *see also* disabled

advocate
A person who shows public support or campaigns for a specific cause and encourages others to do the same.

agenda
A plan of the proposed actions that a person, organization, business, or political party intends to take. Political parties share their political agendas with the public before an election.

Air Quality Index (AQI)
A numbered index from 1 to 500 that shows the level of air pollution at a location. A high AQI value indicates greater health risks.

ally
An individual who stands for and with those who are treated unfairly because of who they are. Allies may or may not experience the type of hardship or discrimination that they are standing against.

anatomy
The structure of the body or of a body part.

app
A computer software program that runs on an electronic device, such as a mobile phone or tablet. Short for application.

asylum
The protection given by a country to a displaced person or people who have left their own country because of reasons beyond their control, such as war, genocide, violence, persecution, discrimination, or natural disasters. *see also* refugee

authoritarianism
A political system in which one person has absolute power over a country and its citizens, often without a constitution in place. An example is a dictatorship. *see also* dictatorship

bias
Prejudice or discrimination against a person, group, community, or belief system, which can result in unfair and unequal treatment. *see also* unconscious bias

biodegradable
A substance that can be broken down by microorganisms to become part of the natural environment.

biodiversity
The variety of animals, plants, and microorganisms that live in a particular area or habitat. Some habitats are more biodiverse than others.

biological sex
The physical characteristics with which a person is born. *see also* gender, gender expression, and gender identity

boycott
To show disapproval or dislike of a company, shop, or system by refusing to use its goods or services and encouraging others to do the same.

brush dam
Structure made of dry branches, twigs, and bushy vegetation to hold loose soil in place.

bullying
Cruel actions, words, or behavior that is meant to mentally or physically intimidate or harm another person.

bushland
Uncultivated land that is covered with trees, shrubs, or other types of plants.

campaigner
see advocate

capitalism
An economic system in which citizens can own wealth and property, ideally without government involvement. However, governments do get involved, making most capitalist economies mixed.

carbon
An element found in all living things on Earth and also in many nonliving materials. Carbon flows through the air, water, and ecosystems on land as the gas carbon dioxide.

carbon dioxide
A gas produced by the respiration of organisms, the fermentation of dead matter, and by the burning of fuels. It is a major greenhouse gas and the main reason behind global warming. *see also* greenhouse effect, global warming, and climate change

carbon footprint
The amount of carbon dioxide released in the atmosphere by the activities of a person, an organization, or a country.

carbon sink
A reservoir that absorbs carbon dioxide from Earth's atmosphere. The two largest carbon sinks are forests and oceans.

caste
A strict social group into which a person is born, according to Hinduism. Some believe that a person's caste determines their position in society.

champion
see advocate

chronic
A health condition that has lasted, or is expected to last, for some time but is not necessarily life-threatening.

citizen
A legally recognized member of a country. *see also* global citizen

citizenship
The state of being a citizen and legally belonging to a country.

civil society
The local communities and groups, private businesses and industries, and non-governmental organizations of a country.

class system
A social system that splits citizens into different groups based on their social and economic positions. This can lead to classism, which is discrimination against people because of their class.

climate change
Changes in climate on Earth due to global warming. Climate change makes it harder for all organisms to live on Earth. *see also* global warming and greenhouse effect

colonialism
The action of one country taking over another by seizing control of their land and people.

colorism
A type of racism in which people, usually from the same race, are treated differently because of how light or dark their skin is. *see also* race and racism

community
The people around an individual make up their community. This may include family, friends, neighbors, classmates, teachers, and other social groups.

compost
A pile of organic waste, such as fruit and vegetable peelings, that breaks down over a period of time into a rich mix of nutrients that can aid in plant growth.

consent
A voluntary agreement to do something or to allow something to happen, such as an intimate emotional or physical relationship.

constituency
An area of a country from where a representative is chosen for the national legislature.

constitution
The set of rules, written or unwritten, that spells out how a country should be governed and what rights its citizens have.

consumer
A person who buys goods or uses the services available in a country.

contraception
A range of methods that can be used to prevent pregnancy. There are two types: barrier and hormone-based. Also called birth control.

crowdsourcing
A process where ideas, information, and services can be sourced from a large group of people online.

cruelty-free
Manufacturing processes for products that do not involve testing them on animals.

cyberbullying
The use of technology to bully people, often online. Examples include sending them threatening emails and messages, sharing their personal photos or information, and taking over their online identity by creating a fake profile.

democracy
A political system in which the people of a country elect representatives who govern the country on their behalf.

desertification
The spread of desert regions to previously fertile lands due to hot and dry weather, droughts, deforestation, and overgrazing.

dictatorship
A type of authoritarianism. In this political system, a leader called a dictator does not allow any form of opposition.

disabled
A person who has a physical, mental, or sensory condition that can affect their everyday activities. *see also* ableism

discrimination
Treating a person unfairly as a result of prejudice, for reasons including age, race, ethnicity, religion, ability, gender identity, and sexual identity.

diversity
Refers to variety. Diversity can mean the presence of a variety of people in society with different identities, backgrounds, and experiences. *see also* inclusion

divine
Relating to a deity, such as a god or goddess.

ecosystem
A biological community of living things that interact with each other in a shared environment.

emission
The release of a gas into the air.

empathy
The ability to understand how someone is feeling.

empowered
Describes the feeling of strength experienced by individuals or groups when there are positive changes in their lives.

endangered
A species of plant or animal that has low numbers or decreasing presence in the wild and runs the risk of disappearing completely. *see also* extinct

endorphins
Chemicals released by the brain that make us feel happy. They can help us manage stress or pain.

entrepreneur
A person who sets up a business.

equality
The idea that everyone should be treated fairly and have the same status, rights, and opportunities.

equity
Adapting support to a person's needs or situation so they have the best chance of fair access to opportunities.

erosion
A process in which soil or rock is broken down and carried away by wind, flowing water, or ice.

ethical
Considering the moral principles of what is right and wrong in order to adopt a fair approach.

ethnicity
Refers to a social identity that is often based on shared culture, such as languages, beliefs, practices, and common ancestry. This is also closely related to the idea of national identity. Ethnicity is learned and passed down through generations. *see also* race

executive
One of the three branches of a democratic government. The executive enforces laws made by the legislature. *see also* judiciary and legislature

extinct
When a species disappears completely due to the death of the last individual.

feminism
The view that men and women should be treated equally, and the movements for addressing women's inequality in society.

food chain
A chain of organisms in which those at one level eat others. For example, a bird of prey may eat insect-eating birds, which in turn eat insects, which in turn feed on the nectar of some flowers.

fossil fuel
A fuel produced from the remains of plants and animals that died millions of years ago. Examples include coal, oil, and natural gas.

freshwater reserve
A source of naturally occurring water that isn't sea or ocean water.

gay
Refers to people who are romantically and sexually attracted to people of the same sex. *see also* homosexual and LGBTQ+

gender
A potential combination of a person's biological sex, gender identity, and gender

expression. Gender can be nonbinary, and not just limited to "male" and "female."

gender dysphoria
The emotional and mental distress that a person experiences when their body does not match their gender identity. *see also* biological sex, gender expression, and gender identity

gender expression
How someone expresses their gender identity outwardly. *see also* gender identity

gender identity
A person's sense of their gender, which may or may not match the gender they were assigned at birth based on their biological sex. An individual may identify as one or more of many different genders. *see also* biological sex, gender, and gender expression

global citizen
A member of humanity. *see also* citizen

global citizenship
The state of being a global citizen. Global citizenship goes beyond national borders. *see also* citizenship

globalization
The process by which people, goods, and businesses across the world are becoming more connected and interdependent.

global warming
The gradual increase in Earth's average temperature due to an enhanced greenhouse effect. Global warming leads to climate change. *see also* greenhouse effect and climate change

green consumerism
The demand for environmentally friendly or recycled goods that do not harm the planet and protect its limited resources.

greenhouse effect
The process in which heat from the sun is trapped in Earth's atmosphere by gases such as carbon dioxide and methane. Rising levels of these gases are enhancing the greenhouse effect, causing global warming. *see also* global warming and climate change

greenhouse gas
A gas that traps heat in Earth's atmosphere. A major example is carbon dioxide. Other examples are methane and nitrous oxide.

habitat
A natural environment that is home to specific types of animal and plant.

hashtag
A pound sign (#) followed by a keyword that collects information or posts on the keyword or topic to make it easier for people to find it online. Hashtags are commonly used on social media platforms. *see also* social media

heatwave
Long period of sustained high temperatures.

heterosexism
The assumption that everyone is straight, based on the prejudiced belief that heterosexual people are "normal" while LGBTQ+ people are "abnormal." *see also* gay, heterosexual, homosexual, LGBTQ+, and straight

heterosexual
A person who is romantically and sexually attracted to a member of the opposite sex. *see also* straight

hierarchy
Different levels in society, usually based on factors such as race, ethnicity, caste, gender, education, wealth, and occupation.

homophobia
Attitudes and behavior that display dislike, distrust, fear, hatred, or bullying of people of the LGBTQ+ community on the basis of their sexual or gender identity.

homosexual
A person who is romantically and sexually attracted to a member of the same sex. *see also* gay

identity
The combination of the different parts of a person's self, including their ideas, values, experiences, beliefs, interests, and gender and sexual identity, that makes them a unique individual.

inclusion
The fair and equal treatment of a diverse set of people in society. *see also* diversity

indigenous people
Groups of culturally and ethnically distinct people who are native to a particular region of the world.

inflation
An increase in the prices of goods and services over a period of time, which makes it difficult for people to buy the things they need with the same amount of money.

infrastructure
The buildings, bridges, roads, railways, and sewers that make up all cities, towns, and villages.

Internet
A massive global network created by using connections between billions of computer and other devices. It is a huge source of information and allows us to socialize with others and build online communities to achieve shared goals. *see also* social media

intersectional feminism
A branch of feminism that takes into account the parts of a person's identity, such as race, ethnicity, social class, and sexual identity, that combine with gender to affect a person's position in society.

intersectionality
The overlapping of different parts of a person's identity, such as ethnicity, class, gender identity, and sexual identity. It may produce unique forms of discrimination and privilege.

invasive species
A species of plant or animal that is not native to a particular ecosystem. It may be a threat to the living things in that environment and may affect their survival.

judiciary
One of the three branches of a democratic government. The judiciary interprets laws in courts. *see also* executive and legislature

jury
A group of people chosen from the general public who are tasked with hearing a court case to provide a fair and unbiased verdict on the basis of the evidence presented.

legislature
One of the three branches of a democratic government. The legislature creates news laws. *see also* executive and judiciary

LGBTQ+
Short for Lesbian, Gay, Bisexual, Trans, questioning, and others. Refers to the entire community of people who identify as any sexual identity other than straight or any nonbinary gender identity. *see also* gender identity and sexual identity

malnutrition
A health condition caused by consuming food, over a long period, that does not contain the right balance of nutrients. Also known as undernourishment.

marginalization
To treat some individuals or groups unfairly and to give them limited access to the rights, resources, and privileges enjoyed by the rest of the population.

misinformation
Inaccurate or deliberately false information presented as fact. Misinformation is common on the Internet. Also known as fake news. *see also* Internet

misogyny
The hatred of and prejudice toward women.

mood swings
Sudden and unpredictable changes in mood, which are common and normal in teenagers.

multiculturalism
The state of people from different cultures living alongside one another in a society.

netizen
A person who uses the Internet frequently.

oil blocks
Geographical areas that have been set aside for oil drilling.

organic
Plants or animals that are grown or reared naturally, without the use of chemicals.

ozone layer
A layer in Earth's atmosphere that absorbs most of the harmful ultraviolet radiation from the sun.

pandemic
A large-scale outbreak of a disease that affects countries and communities all across the world.

peatland
Regions where waterlogged conditions prevent the complete decomposition of plant and other organic matter. This matter accumulates over time and acts as a carbon sink.

peer pressure
A social pressure felt by individuals to be a certain way to fit in with their peers or friends.

period
When the lining of the uterus is discharged from the body with blood as part of a person's monthly menstruation cycle. It is also known as menstruation. Short for menstrual period.

persecution
Oppression or mistreatment of individuals or groups of people.

photosynthesis
The process by which plants take energy from sunlight and use it to convert carbon dioxide and water into food in the form of a sugar called glucose. Oxygen is released as a by-product.

piracy
Illegally downloading or distributing someone's work without their permission.

pollination
The transfer of pollen from a male part of a plant to a female part of a plant for plants to produce new seeds.

pollution
The introduction of harmful substances to the environment, usually due to unchecked human activity.

prejudice
Preconceived ideas or beliefs that are not based in fact and are often untrue and unjust.

pressure group
A group of people committed to raising awareness and gathering support for a specific cause in order to make the government aware of the issue and hopefully take action.

privilege
The often unearned advantages or preference given to some individuals or groups.

propaganda
Biased information meant to promote a person's point of view or cause.

puberty
A period of transition and growth before reaching adulthood.

race
A social idea that is used to distinguish between groups of people based on physical differences, such as skin color. Race has been used by powerful groups to justify the different, and often oppressive, treatment of other groups of people.

racism
The wrong belief that certain races, ethnicities, and skin colors are superior to others.

refugee
Displaced people who have been granted safety or refuge in another country. *see also* asylum

rehabilitation
Returning to full health or everyday life with the help of training and therapy programs.

segregation
The separation of individuals or groups of people based on race, ethnicity, or nationality.

sexism
Prejudice or discrimination against an individual or group due to their gender identity.

sexual harassment
Unwanted, inappropriate, or abusive behavior that is sexual in nature.

sexual identity
How a person identifies themselves based on who they are attracted to emotionally, romantically, and sexually and how they express these attractions. *see also* gay and straight

sexuality
The feelings, thoughts, preferences, behaviors, experiences, and beliefs that a person has related to sex and sexual attraction.

social media
Websites and apps that allow people to share content and interact in online communities.

spam
Unwanted and potentially harmful advertisements, messages, or emails.

stereotype
Someone's oversimplified, untrue assumption that all people who belong to a group have the same traits, without considering the people as individuals.

straight
Refers to people who are romantically and sexually attracted to people of the opposite sex. *see also* heterosexual

suffrage
The right to vote in an election.

sustainability
Meeting the needs of present generations for food, energy, health, and housing in ways that will allow future generations to meet theirs too.

trolling
Threatening, abusive, or insulting messages sent anonymously online with the deliberate intention of provoking a reaction from other people.

unconscious bias
Racist, stereotypical, and discriminatory views held or actions taken by a person without even realizing it.

Index

Acknowledgments

The publisher would like to thank the following people for their help with making the book: Claire Wardle, PhD (Co-founder and US Director of First Draft) for permission to adapt information on "The Different Types of Mis- and Disinformation"; the Economist Intelligence Unit for data from "Democracy Index 2020: In sickness and in health?"; Sanya Jain for design assistance; Nayan Keshan and Vatsal Verma for editorial assistance; Saloni Singh, Priyanka Sharma, and Harish Aggarwal for the jacket; Caroline Stamps for proofreading; and Elizabeth Wise for the index.

The publisher would like to thank the following for their kind permission to reproduce their photographs:

(Key: a-above; b-below/bottom; c-center; f-far; l-left; r-right; t-top)

26-27 KidsRights foundation: Mohamad Aljounde / Gharsah Sweden. **34-35 Shutterstock.com:** Olamikan Gbemiga / AP. **38 Alamy Stock Photo:** Michele and Tom Grimm. **46-47 Shutterstock. com:** Startraks. **47 Alamy Stock Photo:** Cal Vornberger. **51 Alamy Stock Photo:** Martin Heitner / Stock Connection Blue. **54 Dreamstime.com:** Brphoto. **55 123RF.com:** stillfx (tc/background). **Alamy Stock Photo:** WENN Rights Ltd (clb). **Shutterstock.com:** John Gomez (tc). **61 Dreamstime.com:** Monkey Business Images. **65 Shutterstock.com:** Pichayanon Pairojana. **66 Getty Images:** Toshifumi Kitamura / AFP. **75 Shutterstock.com:** Jerry Lampen / EPA. **76 Getty Images:** Stuart Franklin. **78 Getty Images:** Saul Loeb / AFP. **78-79 Maya Terro / FoodBlessed. 79 Maya Terro / FoodBlessed. 82 Getty Images:** Rodrigo Buendia / AFP. **83 123RF.com:** stillfx (cra/background). **Alamy Stock Photo:** Mark Fox (cla). **Getty Images:** Rodrigo Buendia / AFP (cra). **88 Getty Images:** Munir Uz Zaman / AFP. **89 123RF.com:** stillfx (tr/background). **Alamy Stock Photo:** BJ Warnick / Newscom (cl); Suvra Kanti Das / ZUMA Press, Inc. (tr). **90 Association of Southeast Asian Nations (ASEAN):** (br). **United Nations (UN):** © United Nations 2021 (crb). **92 Getty Images:** Haakon Mosvold Larsen / POOL / AFP. **93 Shutterstock. com:** Nicolas Economou / NurPhoto. **97 Science Photo Library:** British Crown Copyright, The Met Office. **98 Getty Images:** Chip Somodevilla. **98-99 Shutterstock.com:** Gian Ehrenzeller / EPA-EFE. **103 Getty Images:** Maskot. **106 Getty Images:** Tony Karumba / AFP. **106-107 Madison Stewart:** Perrin James. **107 Madison Stewart:** @ caraghcreative. **110 Getty Images:** David Gray. **111 Bureau of Meteorology, Australia (www.bom.gov.au):** Reproduced by permission of Bureau of Meteorology, © 2021 Commonwealth of Australia (cl). **Shutterstock.com:** David Mariuz / EPA-EFE (cr). **112 Dreamstime.com:** Jason Gong. **114 Getty Images:** Munir Uz Zaman / AFP. **117 Dreamstime.com:** Ratthpon Chaithawin. **118 Salvador Gómez-Colón:** (cl). **118-119 Salvador Gómez-Colón. 119 Salvador Gómez-Colón. 121 Getty Images:** Education Images / Universal Images Group. **123 Kids against plastic:** Amy and Ella Meek. **127 Alamy Stock Photo:** Jeffrey Isaac Greenberg 7+. **130-131 Shutterstock.com:** Ico Maker. **131 Alamy Stock Photo:** Shelly Rivoli. **132 Getty Images:** Remko De Waal / ANP / AFP. **133 Council of Europe:** No Hate Speech Movement. **143 Kids Caregivers / Hailey Richman. 145 Mr. Matté. 146 Mr. Matté:** (cr)

Endpaper images: *Front and Back:* **123RF.com:** noppadol thammatorn b

All other images © Dorling Kindersley
For further information see: **www.dkimages.com**